Tug boats on the Piscataqua River, Portsmouth

EUGENIA MORAN

The Mount Washington Cog Railway is a National Historic Engineering Landmark. Its first locomotive, Old Peppersass, reached the summit of Mount Washington on July 3, 1869, making it the world's first mountain climbing railroad using a toothed cogwheel to engage the rack between the rails.

David Brownell

New Hampshire
FIRST IN THE NATION

A Photographic Tribute to the Granite State

The Mountain View Grand in Whitefield is one of New Hampshire's oldest grand hotels and one of just four in the state that remain from the 19th century, when hundreds of luxurious accommodations hosted the well-to-do during their summer visits, particularly to the White Mountains.

Marcy and Jerry Monkman

Lancaster native John Wingate Weeks would go on to serve in the U.S. House of Representatives and the U.S. Senate. He crafted the landmark Weeks Act in 1911, which laid the foundation for the country's national park system. His summer home, atop Mount Prospect, is now a New Hampshire state park.

New Hampshire: First In The Nation
A Photographic Tribute to the Granite State

Publisher: Joe Zwiebel
Project Director: Andrea Kolden
Editor: Lorna Colquhoun
Writers: Melanie Plenda, Cissy Taylor
Photo Editor: Russ Rocknak
Design and Production Director: Mitchell Hayes

Distributed by New England Business Media
172 Shrewsbury Street, Worcester, MA 01604

Printed in the U.S.A. by Taylor Specialty Books, Naugatuck, CT

Contents

A bronze statue of Hillsborough native Franklin Pierce, the 14th president of the United States, stands in front of the New Hampshire Statehouse in Concord.

Welcome

Dear Friends:

With our rich history and culture, beautiful natural environment and low taxes, New Hampshire is a unique and wonderful place to live, work and play.

We in New Hampshire take pride in our high quality of life. New Hampshire is consistently named the most livable state in the nation, the safest state and the best state in which to raise children. Our diverse economy, educated workforce and excellent schools make this a great place to raise a family and to do business.

And every four years the national spotlight shines brightly on New Hampshire as we host the First-in-the-Nation presidential primary.

New Hampshire's unique character is punctuated by our breathtaking landscapes – majestic mountains and forests, and clear, cool waters. There are picturesque villages and vibrant cities, which boast a variety of cultural, entertainment and fine dining experiences. As you will see for yourself in the pages of this book, from the Seacoast to the North Country, from the Connecticut River Valley to the Southern Tier – New Hampshire offers something for everyone.

With so much to offer, it is no wonder more and more people are making New Hampshire their destination – whether it's for vacation or for a lifetime.

It is my hope you will take the time to come and experience the advantages of the Granite State for yourself. I can guarantee you will not be disappointed.

Sincerely ,

John H. Lynch

John H. Lynch
Governor

Market Square, Portsmouth

Wentworth-Coolidge Mansion, Portsmouth

A Tour of New Hampshire

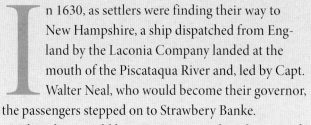

In 1630, as settlers were finding their way to New Hampshire, a ship dispatched from England by the Laconia Company landed at the mouth of the Piscataqua River and, led by Capt. Walter Neal, who would become their governor, the passengers stepped on to Strawbery Banke.

This place would become Portsmouth and as one of the Granite State's first settlements, it is appropriate that we begin our tour here, before setting out for the North Country and exploring what's in between on our way back to where we began.

Seven distinct regions spanning 10 counties comprise New Hampshire - The Seacoast, Dartmouth-Lake Sunapee, the Monadnock Region, the Lakes Region, the Merrimack Valley, the White Mountains and the Great North Woods.

Together, they give the state a richly diverse social and geographical landscape, where its residents enjoy life in an area that is classically New England - small towns, vibrant cities, natural beauty and four seasons.

Powering the state's economy is manufacturing, technology, tourism and agriculture, industries that have a long tradition in the Granite State, fueled by the pride and fierce determination those first settlers had as they stepped on to Strawbery Banke.

New Hampshire offers the distinct geographical ability to spend the morning skiing in the mountains and finish the day with a walk on the Atlantic coast. Its cities and towns appear regularly in national rankings as the best places to live, raise a family and retire.

For those who live here - the Granite Staters - New Hampshire is home, a place where they know their neighbors and where they still celebrate the things that were so important to the first families who called it home - harvest festivals, community suppers, the Fourth of July.

And every four years, the nation shines a spotlight on New Hampshire, the Live Free or Die state, where the first votes are cast for the president of the United States of America.

Join us on our journey through the Granite State.

Philip Cohen

The Tall Ships, Portsmouth

Market Square, Portsmouth

Clapboards, Portsmouth

Governor John Langdon House, Portsmouth

Freighter in Portsmouth

The Music Hall, Portsmouth

Marco Polo, Portsmouth

Boston -Portsmouth Airshow, Pease ANGB - Portsmouth

Brazo, Pleasant Street, Portsmouth

USS Albacore AGSS 569 at the Albacore Museum, Portsmouth

Portsmouth Naval Shipyard, Portsmouth

Rye Harbor

Hampton Beach State Park

Wentworth by the Sea Hotel & Spa, Newcastle

Portsmouth's Smuttynose Brewing Company's owner, Peter Egelston

Bob Lussier

The Crew at Smuttynose Brewing Company, Portsmouth

Bob Lussier

Beer voodoo performed daily at the Smuttynose Brewing Company, Portsmouth

The Bedford Village Inn, Bedford

The Bedford Village Inn's garden, Bedford

Bedford Village Inn's Great Hall and Silos

Bedford Village Inn's Great Hall during the Holidays

Downtown Manchester

Manchester-Boston Regional Airport

The Palace Marquee, Manchester

FIRST Robotics, Manchester

Mill Buildings, Manchester

Downtown Manchester

Currier Museum of Art, Manchester

Currier Museum of Art, Manchester

Currier Museum of Art, Manchester

Currier Museum of Art, Manchester

THE HENRY AND HYLDA SILVER GALLERY

Currier Museum of Art, Manchester

Frank Lloyd Wright's Zimmerman House, Currier Museum of Art, Manchester

Frank Lloyd Wright's Zimmerman House, Currier Museum of Art, Manchester

Frank Lloyd Wright's Zimmerman House, Currier Museum of Art, Manchester

Frank Lloyd Wright's Zimmerman House, Currier Museum of Art, Manchester

The Verizon Center, Manchester

The Manchester Monarchs

The Manchester Monarchs

The Manchester Monarchs

New Hampshire Motor Speedway, Loudon

New Hampshire Motor Speedway, Loudon

New Hampshire Motor Speedway, Loudon

Photo: Peter Finger

Racing fans at the New Hampshire Motor Speedway, Loudon

LACONIA
BB

got lobstah?
Makris
Seafood & Steak House

Tony Stewart wins the Sylvania 300 at New Hampshire Motor Speedway in Loudon

The Fisher Cats playing at the Northeast Delta Dental Stadium, Manchester

The Tilt'n Diner, Tilton: The Common Man Family of Restaurants

The Common Man Family of Restaurants

The Common Man Family of Restaurants

The Airport Diner, Manchester: The Common Man Family of Restaurants

The Common Man Family of Restaurants

State House in Concord

STATE CAPITOL

The State Capitol Building of New Hampshire was built in 1816-19 by Stuart J. Park. It is constructed of New Hampshire granite quarried in Concord. The original part was occupied June 2, 1819 and is the nation's oldest State Capitol in which a legislature meets in its original chambers.

Franklin Pierce statue in front of the Concord State House

Concord State House, Senate

John Hale statue in front of the Concord State House

Icons of
History

Objects that Define
New Hampshire

New Hampshire
Historical Society

The Tuck Library

CLOSED

NEW HAMPSHIRE
HISTORICAL
SOCIETY

New Hampshire Historical Society, Concord

Legislative Office Building, Concord

Museum of New Hampshire History, Concord

Dartmouth Hitchcock Medical Center, Hanover

Revolution Energy, Dover

McAuliffe-Shepard Discovery Center, Concord

Downtown Concord

CONCORD COACH SOCIETY

SILVER RANCH

The Concord Coach Society

Dartmouth College, Hanover

The University of New Hampshire, Durham

The University of New Hampshire's mascot, the Wildcat

The University of New Hampshire's Marching Band

The University of New Hampshire's Wildcats

The University of New Hampshire's Wildcats

The University of New Hampshire's Equine Studies

Fireworks light up the night sky over Boulder Field at The University of New Hampshire, Durham

Keene State College's Alumni Gates, Keene

Keene State College, Keene

Squam Lakes

Julian Duchene climbing Predator at Rattlesnake Mountain in Rumney

Kayaking on Pontook Reservoir with a moose

Mt. Washington Hotel & Presidential Range, Bretton Woods

Cog Railway on Jacob's Ladder, Mt. Washington

David Brownell

Mt. Washington Auto Road

Station

CRAWFORD'S

Conway Scenic Railroad, Crawford Notch Station

The Balsams Grand Resort, Dixville Notch

DIXVILLE NOTCH
"First in the Nation"

New Hampshire has held the first-in-the-nation presidential primaries since 1920. With the first presidential "beauty contest" in 1952, our citizens have personally met the candidates and by popular ballot have declared their preference for their party's nominee. Since 1960, Dixville has been the first community in the state and country to cast its handful of votes in national elections. On election eve 100% of the eligible voters gather in the Ballot Room of The BALSAMS. At midnight polls open and a few minutes later promptly close. The results are broadcast around the world.

Dixville Notch, First in the Nation

Dixville Notch, First in the Nation

The Four Seasons

Sleigh Ride, Nestlenook Farm, Jackson

First Baptist Church, North Conway

Barn in Andover

Tobogganing in Andover

Schouler Park Skating Rink, North Conway

First Baptist Church, Schoular Park and Mt. Cranmore, North Conway

Jackson Covered Bridge, Jackson

Tuckerman's Ravine, Mt. Washington

View of Mt. Lafayette from Cannon Mt., Franconia Notch

Bob Grant

Mt.Washington Observatory

Cannon Mountain

Skiing Cannon Mountain with the Franconia Range as a backdrop

Snowmobiling, Great North Woods, Berlin

Snowboarding Cannon Mountain with the Franconia Range as a backdrop

Snowy Pier, Portsmouth

The Shed, Portsmouth

Portsmouth Harbor Light

Profiles in Excellence

Companies listed by year founded

The City of Rochester

Parson Main graces Central Square in the heart of downtown Rochester.

Rochester combines the charm of a traditional New England city with the energy and vitality of a community focused on the future. Located on the banks of the Cocheco River, Rochester has been home to manufacturing industries since the early 1800s.

"It has a historic downtown with an iconic gazebo, friendly residents and a legacy of textile manufacturing," said Karen Pollard, the city's economic development manager.

The demands of the Civil War led to the formation of the Cocheco Manufacturing Company in 1863, which made woolen blankets for soldiers. By the turn of the 20th century, Rochester bustled with manufacturing industries, such as woolen mills and shoe factories. Four railroads carried out the manufactured goods and carried in tourists and businessmen.

Those industries have been replaced with today's Smart Manufacturing High Technology (SMHT) firms, including Spaulding Composites, Inc., Newport Computers, Phase II Medical and Albany Engineered Composites, which have found opportunities to grow and succeed in Rochester's business friendly environment. With eight industrial parks, the city is positioned to attract more SMHT companies.

Albany Engineered Composites expanded its facility and relocated its international headquarters to Rochester, bringing with it hundreds of high-paying jobs.

"It's a spirit of collaboration, a genuine understanding of what it means to be partner, and just an agile, un-bureaucratic approach to problem solving," which attracted the company to the city, said CEO and president Joe Morone.

Expanding a world-class company requires a world-class workforce. Several educational centers help local industries and manufacturers keep their competitive edge by offering classes to keep their employees on top of technology and other advances in their professions. In nearby Durham, the University of New Hampshire has launched several business and industry programs, including the Innovation Research Center and the High-Tech Accelerator. Great Bay Community College provides customized training for new and expanding companies.

Spaulding High School, serving 1,600 students, is home to the Richard W. Creteau Regional Technology Center, with its career and technical education programs in business, trades occupations and healthcare. It partners with Great Bay Community College to offer adult credit and non-credit courses. The Greater Rochester Chamber of Commerce sponsors business networking, education and other programs for its members.

Rochester is connected to northern New England by a network of air, highway, rail and water routes. The Spaulding Turnpike, a stretch of NH Route 16, is a four-lane highway with six entrances to the city, providing easy access to Interstate 95, the Pease International Tradeport in Portsmouth, Logan Airport in Boston, the Manchester-Boston Regional Airport, the Portland International Jetport and the Port of Portsmouth. The New Hampshire Northcoast Railroad and Skyhaven Airport also serve the city.

The $135 million upgrade of the Spaulding Turnpike spurred commercial and retail expansion. The 675-acre Granite Ridge Development District, adjacent to the turnpike, is the city's largest dedicated commercial and hospitality zone. Rochester Crossing, at exit 13, boasts 300,000-square-feet of retail space, with a 95 percent occupancy rate.

While looking to the future, the city has carefully preserved its past, including the Rochester Opera House, built in 1908. Located on the second and third floors of City Hall, the Opera House has been the center of culture for decades. It is uniquely designed, with a floor that can be raised for performances and lowered for dances and meetings, and it is one of the last of its kind in the country.

Complementing the growing city is affordable housing, from riverfront properties to rural neighborhoods and hilltop homes with spectacular views. Residents can easily travel to the ocean, lakes and mountains and the combination of a quality lifestyle, natural beauty and economic diversity retains companies and their employees.

There are a number of events throughout the year, including the legendary Rochester Fair, a September tradition since

Downtown festivals attract artists and artisans for unique New Hampshire made products.

1892. Downtown merchants host many family-oriented events including the annual Holiday Parade and Trick or Treat on the Town, Concerts on the Common and rotating art displays and walking tours.

Roger Allen Park is one of the best ballparks in New England, boasting one football, five softball, five soccer and 10 baseball fields that accommodate youth activities in the city and the New England region. In addition, baseball fans watch the Seacoast Mavericks, a member of the Futures Collegiate Baseball League, at Spaulding High School's Bert George Field.

"The city of Rochester is a wonderful community filled with caring and compassionate citizens," said Mayor T. J. Jean. "Many families and businesses choose to locate in Rochester because it is a great place to live, work and play."

"The city of Rochester is a wonderful community filled with caring and compassionate citizens," said Mayor T. J. Jean. "Many families and businesses choose to locate in Rochester because it is a great place to live, work and play."

Sulloway & Hollis, PLLC

Over the years, Sulloway has become known as one of the leading law firms in New Hampshire – its lawyers participating in all aspects of law, government and community service.

Sulloway trial attorneys outside the firm's Capitol Street offices.

Sulloway & Hollis, formed in Concord in 1852, traces its roots to the partnership of two Dartmouth College graduates – Anson Marshall and Henry Rolfe. Over the past 160 years, it has helped to form, and represented, many New Hampshire banks, railroads, public utilities and other businesses.

Sulloway attorneys consistently have handled some of the most preeminent cases of the day, relating to medical negligence, railroad regulation, corporate taxation, personal injury, insurance, and the battle over New Hampshire's only nuclear power plant at Seabrook. Sulloway lawyers also have long served as trusted and able advisers on corporate, trusts and estates, banking and real estate matters.

Sulloway's ties to the health care profession are longstanding and strong. The firm has represented the New Hampshire Medical Society for many years, establishing a premier reputation in the field of medical malpractice defense and physician and hospital advocacy. For decades, physicians in New Hampshire were represented almost exclusively by two long-time Sulloway partners, Frank J. Sulloway and Irving 'Ted' Soden. That tradition of excellence continues today. As the complexity of the health care industry evolves, Sulloway works to help its physician and hospital clients manage ever-increasing corporate and regulatory requirements.

Over the years, Sulloway has become known as one of the leading law firms in New Hampshire – its lawyers participating in all aspects of law, government and community service. In addition to providing clients with trusted legal advice, Sulloway attorneys have gone on to serve as New Hampshire Chief Justices, associate justices of the state's supreme and superior courts, members of the U.S. Senate and House and the state legislature, and in city government.

Sulloway lawyers have served as governor's counsel and on many other governmental boards and agencies. The firm's lawyers have also undertaken leadership roles in support of the legal profession by service on the boards of or as members of many organizations, including the Board of Bar Examiners, the Professional Conduct Committee, the New Hampshire Bar Association, the Campaign for Legal Services, the American College of Trial Lawyers, the Defense Research Institute, the Federation of Defense and Corporate Counsel and the American Health Lawyers Association.

As a preeminent law firm in northern New England, Sulloway & Hollis offers a wide range of services to its clients. Its lawyers represent businesses, public entities, nonprofit organizations, and individuals in business, regulatory, and litigation matters. Recognizing that all legal issues a client faces do not fall neatly into one practice area, Sulloway lawyers work collaboratively to deliver comprehensive legal solutions tailored to clients' needs.

Sulloway's current practice focuses on health care and medical malpractice defense; labor and employment and school law; litigation; real estate, land use, environmental law and commercial finance; business and corporate law; trusts and estates and probate administration; and domestic relations.

A multidisciplinary and practical approach to problem solving allows Sulloway to represent clients effectively and cost efficiently. The firm primarily serves clients with legal matters in New Hampshire, Vermont, Maine and Massachusetts; its lawyers have appeared in the state and federal courts of all of those states and in the United States Supreme Court.

The long tradition of excellence upheld by Sulloway continues to be recognized by its peers and by organizations that evaluate the performance of law firms.

The firm is rated 'AV', the highest possible ranking, by Martindale-Hubbell Law Directory, the renowned directory of lawyers and law firms in the United States and around the world. Several lawyers also have received the prestigious 'AV' rating.

Chambers USA, a respected legal directory of leading law firms and attorneys in the United States, which bases its guide on independent research and interviews with clients and peers, recognizes Sulloway as a leading U.S. law firm. Each year, many of the firm's lawyers are also recognized in The Best Lawyers

Members of the firm's Trusts and Estates and Labor and Employment Groups advise clients in the firm's Concord office.

in America, an annual industry referral guide covering all 50 states and the District of Columbia.

Its lawyers are often honored by such national and regional groups as the American College of Trial Lawyers, New England Super Lawyers and the American College of Labor and Employment Lawyers.

In addition to its outstanding legal work, Sulloway plays an active role in the New Hampshire business community, participating in many local and statewide organizations, like the Greater Concord Chamber of Commerce, the Business and Industry Association and other organizations that work to promote Concord's and New Hampshire's continued economic prosperity.

Sulloway and its employees also support many charitable and nonprofit organizations that help make New Hampshire a better place to live. The firm is particularly proud of its support of the arts, regularly showcasing local artists in its Robert M. Larsen Gallery.

"Celebrating Clients and Community" has been Sulloway's motto as it celebrates its 160th anniversary. As the oldest law firm in New Hampshire, Sulloway is proud of its past but is committed to the future and to continued quality representation of its clients and service to Concord and New Hampshire.

The long tradition of excellence upheld by Sulloway continues to be recognized by its peers and by organizations that evaluate the performance of law firms.

St. Paul's School

Many ponds dot the landscape of St. Paul's, including Library Pond, which provides a scenic vista for the Sheldon building, home to the Admission Office.

Peter Finger

In the spring of 1856, a young schoolteacher arrived in a carriage at a large property of ponds and woods near Concord, where a wealthy Boston physician had provided land to create a new school. St. Paul's School began that same day, as three boys received their first assignments, one of which was to go fishing. A love of the school's natural habitat has remained constant since those early days.

If you stand in the center of the St. Paul's School campus today, two things strike you. First is the natural beauty of the place. Tree-lined, brick paths wind their way around the grounds. Serene ponds dot the green grass, providing easy context for that initial assignment, a century and a half later. Next are the buildings - historic, Gothic structures, notably the Chapel of St. Peter and St. Paul, which stands as the literal and figurative heart of the school's tight-knit community. It is here that students and faculty gather four mornings a week for services, announcements, and a way to begin their day together.

Affiliated with the Episcopal Church, St. Paul's School is a co-educational college preparatory boarding school set on a campus of 2,000 wooded acres on the western edge of Concord. In the summer of 2011, Michael G. Hirschfeld, Class of 1985, succeeded the retiring William R. Matthews, 1961, as head of school, becoming the Thirteenth Rector in the school's history.

SPS was a boys' school until 1971, when it became one of the first boarding schools to transition to coeducation, welcoming 19 girls that winter. Today, St. Paul's is one of only a handful of all-boarding schools in the United States.

The grounds are home to approximately 530 young men and women from 37 states and 18 countries. All students and nearly 100 full-time faculty members live on the grounds.

The mission statement reflects the unchanging values of the school: "St. Paul's School is a fully residential academic community that pursues the highest ideals of scholarship. We strive to challenge our students intellectually and morally – to nurture a love for learning and a commitment to engage as servant leaders in a complex world. Founded in the Episcopal tradition, St. Paul's models and teaches a respect for self and others; for one's spiritual, physical, and emotional well-being; for the natural environment; and for service to a greater good."

In the traditional school-year months, St. Paul's School values the highest academic achievement and close student-teacher relationships to provide the quality of the total experience students have in their daily lives.

St. Paul's students are scholars, dancers, skiers, musicians, artists, and athletes. Alumni range from artists such as Pulitzer Prize-winning cartoonist Garry Trudeau, 1966, to civic leaders such as U.S. Senators John Kerry, 1962, and Sheldon Whitehouse, 1973, and current FBI Director Robert Mueller, 1962.

Among the school's facilities are two chapels; 18 dormitories; Ohrstrom Library; Hargate Art Center and Gallery; Oates Performing Arts Center, and the Hawley Astronomy Center, home to the largest telescope in New England. Sports facilities include the 95,000-square-foot Athletic and Fitness Center; the two-rink Matthews Hockey Center; squash and tennis courts; the Crumpacker Boathouse, and a 2,000-meter rowing course. The 78,000-square-foot Lindsay Center for Mathematics and Science will open in 2012 and will feature a solar observatory, 14 laboratories, 21 classrooms and multiple areas for spontaneous collaboration.

St. Paul's is also home to the 55-year-old Advanced Studies Program, which provides five-and-a-half weeks of intensive academic study for rising New Hampshire public and parochial high school seniors. ASP offers academically motivated high school juniors an opportunity to live each summer on the vast St. Paul's School grounds and to immerse themselves in one of 19 areas of study.

In a typical summer, ASP hosts approximately 270 rising seniors from nearly every one of New Hampshire's 85 high schools. Among the course offerings are Artificial Intelligence, Japanese Language and Culture, Mass Media, Biomedical Ethics, Astronomy, and Shakespeare for Performance. One of the newest classes is Introduction to Arabic Language and Culture.

In its more than half a century of existence, ASP has already enriched the academic lives of over 10,000 Granite State students. Many students have been the beneficiaries of the need-based financial aid package, funded solely by donations. In 2011, more than $235,000 in financial assistance was awarded to ASP students, making the program as affordable as possible for New Hampshire families.

Environmental responsibility is something St. Paul's School takes very seriously as a community. Each year since 2007, students have participated in the Green Cup Challenge, which invites schools to measure and reduce campus electricity use and greenhouse gas emissions, while also supporting efforts such as recycling and water conservation.

The new Lindsay Center for Mathematics and Science has been built for LEED certification, an environmental design standard achieved by the Athletic and Fitness Center in 2004. Among the environmentally-conscious features of the Lindsay Center are a sensor system that controls the structure's interior climate, triple-pane windows that reduce heat loss by 50 per-

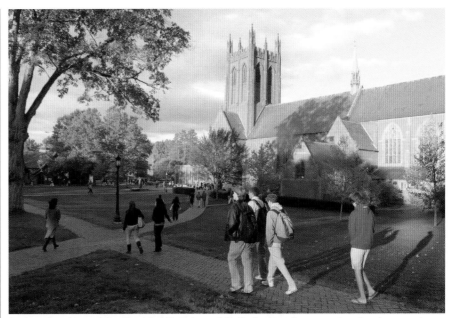

Students head toward the Chapel of St. Peter and St. Paul, where they come together four mornings a week.

cent, solar thermal panels that preheat water, and a photovoltaic system that produces some of the electricity needed at the site. The Lindsay Center is designed to use approximately one-third less energy than traditional buildings of a similar size.

Other recent environmental initiatives include replacing traditional lighting in major campus buildings with high-output fluorescents, a tray-less movement in the dining hall, which has greatly reduced food and water waste, and attaining Energy Star certification for new and renovated faculty houses.

A responsibility to others and a global outlook are fundamental to the school, which requires 40 hours of community service for each student before graduation, and provides numerous opportunities for students to immerse themselves in different cultures through the off-campus programs office and on-campus programming.

In its more than half a century of existence, ASP has already enriched the academic lives of over 10,000 Granite State students.

St. Mary's Bank

The conceptual rendering of the new St. Mary's Bank corporate office. Construction will begin in 2012, with the opening planned for 2013.

St. Mary's Bank, the nation's first credit union, was founded in 1908 in Manchester as "La Caisse Populaire, Ste-Marie" (The People's Bank). At the time, immigrants working in the city's textile mills had no access to traditional deposit and loan accounts. Monsignor Pierre Hevey, Pastor of Ste. Marie's parish in Manchester, along with other community leaders, took the initiative to meet the needs of this underserved population, creating a place that for just $5, anyone could purchase a share, open an account, and begin to save money and obtain loans.

Their revolutionary idea not only succeeded, but sparked a national credit union movement that is now 90 million members strong.

Today, the price of a St. Mary's Bank share is still $5. CEO Ronald H. Covey is just the eighth president in the credit union's 100-plus-year history, which speaks to St. Mary's Bank's tremendous stability and continuity. It's an advantage that has allowed the credit union to focus on what really matters - serving the families, individuals, and businesses of New Hampshire. As a full-service financial provider with over 62,000 members and nine branches, St. Mary's Bank proves time and again the power of great service and affordability.

Readers of New Hampshire Business Review have repeatedly voted St. Mary's Bank "best credit union," and the honor may well have much to do with the institution's continued commitment to "people helping people." Innovating around its century-old mission, St. Mary's Bank has designed programs and products to bring people closer to achieving their dreams, providing opportunities for building and restoring credit, purchasing a first home, opening a first checking account, saving for college and retirement, financing business expansion, and so much more. From financial planning to a seamless home buying process, members expect it all at St. Mary's Bank.

A member-owned and locally managed credit union, St. Mary's Bank has over a century of commercial experience, $700 million in assets, and all the services business require. At the heart of its business division is a local team that understands New Hampshire business dynamics and offers quick turnaround on critical decisions.

"We have always considered supporting local business as one of the key factors in creating healthy communities," says Covey. "That's why we have always taken, and continue to take, the initiative in helping business owners."

St. Mary's Bank embraces a culture of service excellence that is evident whether making a visit to the credit union in person or online. As paperless banking becomes the norm, the credit union has undertaken technology initiatives to make every aspect of banking more convenient, affordable, and secure. Projects are always underway to further enhance mobile and online banking services, improve website usability, update ATMs, and outfit branches with state-of-the-art amenities.

Serving members extends far beyond the credit union's doors to the community at large. Since 1996, St. Mary's Bank has made over $34 million in loans and grants available to underserved New Hampshire families and not-for-profit organizations through its Community Outreach Programs. Countless lower income families and small businesses have benefited from the program's affordable housing, higher education, and community development initiatives. Organizations that have received aid include Big Brothers Big Sisters of Greater Manchester; Boys & Girls Club of Greater Nashua; New Horizons Soup Kitchen and Shelter; Moore Center Services and Currier Museum of Art.

Giving back is a matter of course not just for St. Mary's Bank, but also its employees. Every year, dozens of employees demonstrate their personal commitment to the communities in which they live and work, collectively volunteering many thousands of hours in support of local non-profits and social service agencies. The credit union has been a pacesetter organization for the Granite United Way for many years and was recently recognized for a workplace campaign that raised nearly $50,000.

St. Mary's Bank has been a leader in preserving the history of the credit union movement in the United States. Former CEO Ronald J. Rioux volunteered many hours to help establish America's Credit Union Museum at St. Mary's Bank's first place of business, a private home on Manchester's West Side. The museum, founded in 2002, brings to life a unique time in America's history through personalized accounts and creative exhibits. Its mission is to create an awareness of and appreciation for all that credit unions do.

Just up the street from St. Mary's Bank headquarters is America's Credit Union Museum. It is the site of the credit union's first office operated in the home of Joseph Boivin, 1908 to 1913.

On the first floor of the museum, the offices of the first credit union are recreated in detail, right down to the family parlor that served as the original deposit room and visitors can sit on the long bench where the mill workers once waited to see the president. Second floor exhibits focus on the credit union industry, its strength in hard times, and firsthand accounts from its most important historical figures – credit union members. The third floor is dedicated to education, offering space for seminars and meetings.

Still not-for-profit and member owned today, St. Mary's Bank remains steadfast in its commitment to helping people achieve the lives they envision for themselves. St. Mary's Bank is the place where over 100 years of experience come together with a spirit of innovation and inspiration to create a banking experience unlike any other.

"We have always considered supporting local business as one of the key factors in creating healthy communities."

St. Mary's Bank's first stand-alone building and corporate headquarters from 1930 to 1970.

Business & Industry Association

BIA's Annual Dinner and awards ceremony is New Hampshire's largest business networking event.

Preserving and enhancing the state's business climate—often referred to as the New Hampshire Advantage—is the BIA's top public policy priority.

When legislation is introduced that affects Granite State businesses, the work of lawmakers and state regulators is monitored closely by the Business and Industry Association of New Hampshire.

With a mission to promote a healthy business climate and robust economy for New Hampshire, the BIA, through advocacy with state legislators, the governor and state regulators, shapes business-friendly public policy and provides counterbalance to legislation and regulations that could otherwise threaten the growth and prosperity of the state's business community.

"The BIA is the only broad-based, statewide business advocacy group in New Hampshire," said President Jim Roche, who has led the organization since 2005 following the retirement of long-time President John Crosier. "We are New Hampshire's statewide chamber of commerce and leading business advocate. Our focus is principally on state-level public policy because we understand that the decisions made at the State House directly impact New Hampshire's business climate and the choices of business leaders about where to locate and expand. If we want a healthy economy, we need businesses that create jobs and bring wealth into the state."

The BIA marks its centennial in 2013. It was in 1913 that a group of manufacturers, concerned about government intervention and overregulation of business, formed the New Hampshire Manufacturer's Association. The organization changed its name to the Business and Industry Association in 1970 to reflect its diverse membership and changed its tagline in 2005 to "New Hampshire's statewide chamber of commerce" to reflect its focus on state-level public policy affecting businesses throughout the state. It remains the New Hampshire affiliate of the National Association of Manufacturers.

The BIA represents more than 400 leading employers in a variety of industries including advanced manufacturing, high technology, professional services, financial services, health care, hospitality and tourism, public utilities, higher education and insurance. Member firms employ 86,000 people throughout the state and contribute $4.5 billion annually to the state's economy. It represents companies of various sizes in every region of the state.

Preserving and enhancing the state's business climate—often referred to as the New Hampshire Advantage—is the BIA's top public policy priority. The organization supports fiscally conservative state budgets with a business-friendly tax structure and business tax incentives that foster economic growth.

The organization also works to mitigate rising healthcare and energy costs; increase the availability and affordability of housing for working people; improve pro-business labor rules and regulations that consider the rights and responsibilities of workers and management; expand telecommunications infrastructure throughout the state and balance environmental policies, legislation and administrative rules with the long-term viability of the state's natural resources.

Each year, BIA establishes a proactive business agenda that reflects the top challenges and concerns of New Hampshire's business community. The agenda guides the BIA's legislative efforts as it seeks sensible solutions to business challenges and responds to legislative proposals that may help or harm business in New Hampshire.

In addition to its public policy advocacy, BIA produces substantive forums, conferences and events throughout the year that represent opportunities for members and the greater business community to build relationships and network with one another.

The BIA truly is New Hampshire's statewide chamber of commerce and leading business advocate.

The gold-painted wooden eagle on top of the New Hampshire Statehouse dome was raised in 1818, to the toast of then-Gov. Plumer, who said, "The American Eagle. May the shadow of his wings protect every acre of our united continent and the lightning of his eye flash terror and defeat through the ranks of our enemies."

C&S Wholesale Grocers, Inc.

Our selectors are very important team members when you consider that C&S ships over 1 billion cases of groceries each year.

I n 1918, Israel Cohen and Abraham Siegel bought a small brick warehouse and began delivering groceries to stores in Worcester, Mass. They named their fledgling enterprise "C&S," and worked hard to build a base of loyal, satisfied customers.

Nine decades later, what started as a small warehouse and a handful of employees has become the largest grocery wholesaler in the U.S.

Today, with net sales in excess of $20 billion, C&S is the 10th largest privately held company in the United States, according to Forbes Magazine. With its corporate headquarters in Keene, the company distributes food to supermarkets, retail stores and military bases across the country.

Currently, C&S serves about 3,900 stores from more than

50 locations in 11 states. Among its customers are many of America's best known companies, including Stop & Shop, Giant of Carlisle, Giant of Landover, Great Atlantic & Pacific Tea Co. (A&P), Safeway, Bi-Lo, Tops Friendly Markets, Target and Kroger.

C&S is recognized as a dynamic and progressive leader in the grocery industry, yet is still family owned and operated and committed to delivering the very best in service and quality to its customers. While C&S primarily provides grocery wholesaling and distribution services to the retail grocery industry, C&S also provides third-party logistics solutions to large food manufacturers; operates about 100 retail grocery stores; licenses certain trademarks for use in the retail grocery business, and is developing advanced technologies for use in

C&S then processes orders quickly and efficiently and ships goods expediently to supermarkets, independent retailers and military bases across the country.

C&S is committed to good corporate citizenship and to giving back to the communities where it operates. C&S partners with national nonprofits that address social issues such as hunger, children's literacy and the environment. The company engages employees to make decisions about local requests and encourages them to share their time and talents as volunteers. Each year, the company donates millions of pounds of food to Food Banks which in turn supply community pantries, soup kitchens and other hunger relief organizations.

C&S also helps fund hundreds of civic, charitable and community organizations—from well-known groups like United Way to small, innovative programs with more heart than cash. And when it comes to volunteering, employees give their time and energy to a wide variety of community organizations.

Any company can make a profit, but not every company can make a difference. C&S is committed to doing both.

C&S supports initiatives to stop hunger and to promote the health and enrichment of communities that are homes to its employees and facilities. A corporate social responsibility strategic plan developed in 2008 helped C&S redefine its community commitment.

Chairman & CEO Rick Cohen

The strategy is guiding the company toward building a better values-based company, engaging employees to take action on behalf of others, investing in local community groups, and leveraging its strategic nonprofit partnerships to drive change nationally.

For 25 years, the C&S Wholesale Grocers' charity golf outing, known as "Tee Up for Kids™," has raised millions of dollars to benefit organizations helping children who are battling cancer and, recently, organizations with campaigns addressing childhood hunger and nutrition. Considered one of the largest charity golf tournaments in northern New England, drawing about 900 golfers, the annual event consistently raises over $1 million, which is distributed to highly-respected nonprofit organizations.

Established in 2010, C&S Charities, Inc., is a New Hampshire not-for-profit corporation supporting C&S Wholesale Grocers, Inc's charitable efforts and is is an IRC § 501(c)(3) charitable organization.

For more than 90 years, C&S has been built by the pride, purpose and excellence of its employees and is grateful that thousands of men and women choose to invest their skills and talents as members of the enterprise. Their leadership distinguishes its performance and their value inspires the broader mission as a corporate citizen.

Any company can make a profit, but not every company can make a difference. C&S is committed to doing both.

automated warehouses.

Today, C&S supplies its customers with over 95,000 different products from more than 50 high-tech facilities, delivering everything from seafood to soup to dishwashing liquid. C&S also offers independent retailers a full range of best-in-class store management services to help them run their businesses efficiently and profitably.

As the largest wholesale grocery supply company (by revenue) in the U.S. and the lead supply chain company in the food industry, C&S helps both independently-owned retailers and national supermarket chains procure high-quality, low-cost goods for their customers. C&S operates regional distribution centers throughout the United States, where they receive products from food and grocery producers.

New Hampshire Liquor Commission

Many New Hampshire Liquor and Wine Outlets feature spacious shopping areas with modern lighting to enhance the shopping experience.

A key revenue-generator for the state, the commission's 78 New Hampshire Liquor and Wine Outlets attract visitors from all over the country, grossing sales of more than $500 million annually.

When the first New Hampshire state liquor stores opened in 1934, the United States had just repealed Prohibition, the 13-year ban on the sale, manufacture, and transportation of alcohol nationwide. That year, New Hampshire created the New Hampshire Liquor Commission, an organization that ultimately became an integral part of state business.

Founded to create and manage an effective, state-based system of alcohol regulation and distribution, the NHLC is thriving more than 75 years later. A key revenue-generator for the state, the commission's 78 New Hampshire Liquor and Wine Outlets attract visitors from all over the country, grossing sales of more than $500 million annually. Since 1934, the NHLC has contributed more than $2 billion to the state coffers.

"Every day, I'm mindful that I work for the people of New Hampshire," says NHLC Chairman Joseph Mollica. "All of our employees, from commissioners to in-store sales staff, realize the common goal to serve not only our consumers but all the citizens of our state."

Profits are directed to the state's General Fund, supporting social programs, which in turn benefit all New Hampshire residents. In 2011, a record-breaking $140 million in profits was generated, the largest contribution in the commission's history.

"Our bottom line is important to our business success but we also want to preserve the New Hampshire way of life," said Mollica. "As a control state, our regulatory and safety goals are equally important."

After Prohibition was repealed in 1933, regulation of alcoholic beverages reverted to individual states. Shortly afterward, New Hampshire became one of 18 "control states" – directly controlling the distribution and regulation of alcoholic beverages. In 1934, 15 state liquor stores opened across New Hampshire.

As sole retailer of distilled spirits and sole wholesaler of wine and spirits, the NHLC is charged with regulating the sale of alcohol within the state, as well as licensing. Three commissioners – Mollica, Mark Bodi, and Michael Milligan – appointed by the governor lead the NHLC, overseeing all aspects of the business.

Mollica attributes the NHLC's success to good, solid business principles and responsiveness to customer needs. "Consumers today want great selection and great prices," he said. "Our Liquor and Wine Outlets give them both, in stores that exude a pleasant shopping environment."

The NHLC firmly believes in solid business partnerships with its regional brokers and national suppliers in order to deliver on the promise of everyday low prices to its consumers.

In response to retail trends as well as consumer shopping habits, the commission has made modernization of existing New Hampshire Liquor and Wine Outlets a priority. Stores are renovated, and in some cases, relocated, to visible, more convenient locations. Interior updates, including ergonomic wooden shelving, easier-to-access displays, spacious shopping areas and modern, efficient, visually pleasing lighting, enhance the shopping experience. To showcase the NHLC's vast selection of wines from around the world, some outlets feature wine rooms and tasting areas, a welcoming environment for customers to sample different wines and spirits.

Consumers are excited about the updates and renovations the commission has made at Liquor and Wine Outlets across the state and increased outlet sales prove it.

The NHLC licenses thousands of "on-premise" and "off-premise" establishments, restaurants, inns, resorts, clubs, bars, grocery and convenience stores, that in turn generate millions of dollars in revenue for the state. The commission recognizes licensees as valuable business partners, working closely with them in their hospitality role to promote the state and a New Hampshire way of life.

In addition to generating revenue, the NHLC provides education to licensees, servers and citizens about safe and responsible consumption of alcohol through its Bureau of Enforcement and Licensing. General education programs include: Buyer Beware, an adult education program about the effects of providing alcohol to minors; Ripple Effect, a high school education program about the consequences of driving drunk, and Fatal Choices, a program that uses a DWI simulator to recreate the experience of driving drunk. In response to its outreach efforts, the bureau was named Liquor Law Enforcement Agency of the Year in 2007 by the National Liquor Law Enforcement Association.

In 2008, the NHLC launched the first Impaired Driver Mobile Command Unit, with breathalyzer equipment and a drug recognition expert area, to be used at field sobriety checkpoints throughout New Hampshire to assist state and local police departments. In keeping with the commission's emphasis on regulatory function, community education and building relationships, the Mobile Command Unit is used for programs at New Hampshire schools and to increase general consumer awareness.

The commission collaborates with other state agencies to promote New Hampshire as a tourist destination and a great place to live, work and call home. It's this collaboration that ensures the future success of the NHLC, says Mollica, as well as the innovation and dedication of its staff.

"People often comment about the 'New Hampshire Advantage' – a lifestyle that people here enjoy," Mollica said. "We plan to build on that advantage by expanding access to finer wines and spirits, additional outlet locations and providing continued outstanding customer service."

To showcase the NHLC's vast selection of wines from around the world, some outlets feature wine rooms and tasting areas, for customers to sample different wines and spirits.

Anthem Blue Cross and Blue Shield in New Hampshire

The Anthem Blue Cross and Blue Shield Foundation is a major supporter of the Boys & Girls Clubs of America's (BGCA) Triple Play program which promotes healthy behaviors. Here, members of the Manchester Boys and Girls Club participate in a successful attempt to break the world record for jumping jacks.

Since 1942, Anthem Blue Cross and Blue Shield in New Hampshire has been helping improve the lives of the members it serves and the health of the state. Today, more than a half million Granite Staters rely on Anthem's health products and services and the company proudly serves the entire state and every segment of the health insurance market with New Hampshire-based associates.

In the company's DNA can be found the legacy of three strong organizations: The original Blue Cross and Blue Shield of New Hampshire, founded on Nov. 27, 1942; Matthew Thornton Health Plan, the state's first HMO, which was acquired by BCBSNH in 1997, and Anthem, Inc., a mutual insurance company, which acquired BCBSNH in 1999. Proceeds from the sale of BCBSNH to Anthem BCBS created the Endowment for Health, a statewide, private, nonprofit foundation dedicated to improving the health of New Hampshire's people, especially those who are vulnerable and underserved. Since 2001, the endowment has awarded 755 grants, totaling nearly $32 million to support a wide range of health-related programs and projects in New Hampshire. In 2004, Anthem's parent company merged with WellPoint, Inc.

Today, Anthem Blue Cross and Blue Shield in New Hampshire operates as the state's largest and longest standing insur-er, with a deep local presence, market knowledge and an appreciation for New Hampshire's collaborative environment.

"Our priority is to ensure that our customers have access to affordable, high quality care," said Lisa M. Guertin, Anthem's president. "New Hampshire is a tightly-knit state where all of the stakeholders involved in health care financing and delivery can come together to make a difference."

Marking its 70th year serving New Hampshire, the company, since its inception, has been on the leading edge in helping to keep its members healthy and saving them money.

According to the New Hampshire Center for Public Policy (*What is New Hampshire: A Collection of Data for Those Seeking Answers*, September 2011), health care spending in New Hampshire is 19 percent of its annual Gross Domestic Product , the highest in recent history. That percentage is expected to grow to 24 percent by 2018. As businesses and individuals grapple with the challenge of providing and obtaining affordable health coverage, Anthem is responsive to the needs of those it serves.

By collaborating with providers, Anthem works to ensure its customers have access to affordable, high quality care, through innovative partnerships in which individual providers and hospitals are rewarded based on quality care and positive outcomes. A collaborative with Dartmouth-Hitch-

Anthem is proud to serve as a major sponsor of Bras Across the River in downtown Manchester. The annual event raises funds and awareness to help fight breast cancer in the Granite State.

cock Medical Center focuses on increasing value to patient and slowing the rate of health care cost increases, with an aim at reducing future premium increases. This could lead to the formation of an Accountable Care Organization, defined as an organization of health care providers that agrees to be accountable for the quality, cost and overall care of the health plan members assigned to it.

Anthem works with its employer groups in seeking opportunities to help them "bend the cost curve." Its Site of Service benefit option helps customers identify lower cost providers for a broad range of services, including outpatient surgery and lab work that could reduce or eliminate co-pays.

Anthem's expansive urgent care and walk-in center network across the state allows customers to receive non-emergency care at a fraction of what it would cost in a hospital emergency room, a measure that saves time and money for the treatment of non-life threatening illness and injury.

The Compass SmartShopper program provides customers with financial incentives for choosing lower cost providers for a range of procedures and diagnostic exams. The program creates an informed consumer and reduces claims costs.

Anthem strives to educate and inform consumers through transparency, working to provide them with information and resources to help support healthy decisions for themselves and their families. These efforts include Anthem's Care

Comparison, a tool that enables customers to compare costs on a list of common procedures at New Hampshire hospitals and health care facilities. The My Health Advantage program examines claims from members and identifies health improvement opportunities and the Condition Care Incentive Program, allowing patients to waive co-pays and reduce drug costs for those with chronic conditions who enroll in a disease management program.

"Chronic lifestyle diseases such as diabetes, high blood pressure and heart disease take a devastating toll on New Hampshire," Guertin said. "That's why we provide a broad range of management tools and resources for our customers with these conditions to help them achieve and maintain a healthier lifestyle."

With the New Hampshire State Health Index as a basis, Anthem uses the information to identify and address major health issues in the state. As part of the initiative, the company has formed a dedicated team to work with local and state officials and community organizations, with a goal to research the reasons behind the prevalent health deficiencies and to design policy solutions and implement or enhance programs to improve overall health in the state.

Aside from its daily effort to serve its customers, Anthem has a decades-long tradition of giving back, through charitable contributions and sponsorships, foundation grants and its annual associate giving campaign. It supports a broad range of non-profit programs and activities across the state and its New Hampshire associates volunteer thousands of hours in their local communities. When it comes to charitable giving, Anthem's primary focus is supporting healthier lifestyles and supporting those with chronic conditions.

"Many might think of us primarily as a health benefits company," Guertin said. "But Anthem Blue Cross and Blue Shield in New Hampshire is that and so much more. We're a major private employer with hundreds of New Hampshire-based associates in good jobs. We contribute millions of dollars to the state's economy and our communities each year. Most importantly, we are a company made up of New Hampshire people who care deeply about the state where we live and work."

Aside from its daily effort to serve its customers, Anthem has a decades-long tradition of giving back, through charitable contributions and sponsorships, foundation grants and its annual associate giving campaign.

Each April, in support of agencies across New Hampshire, Anthem associates and their family members take part in Anthem's Community Service Day program.

Community College System of New Hampshire

New Hampshire's community colleges offer a high-quality education that is affordable and accessible

There are seven community colleges in New Hampshire, serving more than 27,000 learners throughout the state.

Community College System of New Hampshire In the changing times that have defined New Hampshire in the 21st century, the state's seven community colleges have stepped forward to meet the challenges, providing key resources, expertise and opportunities as the shifting economic landscape has demanded new and innovative approaches to education.

"Education at all levels, but particularly at the postsecondary level, is the cornerstone of a resilient economy and a healthy civil society," said J. Bonnie Newman, chancellor of the Community College System of New Hampshire. "And now more than ever, for our state to remain competitive, we need a highly skilled, well-educated work force. The demand for the kinds of educational services offered at community colleges has never been greater."

There are seven community colleges in New Hampshire, serving more than 27,000 learners throughout the state. CCSNH includes Great Bay Community College, serving the Seacoast region; Manchester and Nashua Community Colleges, serving two of the state's urban centers; Lakes Region Community College, set amid one of the stunning recreational areas of the state; NHTI-Concord's Community College, serving the Central Capital region; River Valley Community College in Claremont and Keene, covering the western region of the state along the New Hampshire-Vermont border, and White Mountains Community College, serving the vast North Country, from the main campus in Berlin and academic centers in Conway and Littleton.

Learners of all ages, backgrounds and aspirations can take advantage of affordable, high-quality and close-to-home programs that combine general education with sophisticated technical and professional training. The CCSNH is also one of the state's largest providers of online courses, important in this geographically diverse area of population centers and rural communities.

Students can choose from a broad array of academic programs culminating in an associate degree or certificate, whether their goal is to transfer to a baccalaureate institution or continue into a career.

The CCSNH traces its roots back to the end of World War II, when two branch campuses were established as a means to give returning veterans an opportunity for higher education, career training and a path back into civilian life. The hallmark of those early years was a focus on technical and vocational fields, but as the state's economy evolved, so did the community colleges, incorporating technological advances into their curriculum and broadening their scope to include fields like business, education, life sciences, allied health, public safety, hospitality and tourism, social services, engineering and information technology, visual arts and multimedia. The system now is comprised of seven comprehensive and fully accredited community colleges serving every region of the state.

The community colleges strive to be responsive to students' needs and ensure their offerings remain in tune with the economy.

"The community colleges are focused on quality. Students find an academic setting that offers challenges, rigor, and the tools for future success," said Paul Holloway, chairman of the CCSNH Board of Trustees and a long-time business leader in the state.

Students also find vibrant campuses, with clubs and organizations, sports, leadership opportunities, places to network, socialize and pursue their interests outside the classroom.

Businesses both large and small in New Hampshire understand the importance of their local community college and that is why strong partnerships exist between businesses and the colleges. The importance of local connections is what puts the "community" in "community college," as is the fact that many instructors are drawn from the business community and bring the knowledge and perspective of today's skilled workplace.

In 2011, CCSNH embarked on a major initiative to support the growth of the advanced manufacturing sector in New Hampshire. Historically a key driver of the state's economy, manufacturing has transformed into an innovation-based industry using advanced technology, computers, robotics and precision machines and processes. New Hampshire's community colleges, in collaboration with employers and workforce development partners, are creating training programs to meet the need for a highly-skilled workforce for the advanced manufacturing environment.

Programs will address core manufacturing skills, as well as advanced specialized training aligned to regional industry and employment opportunities. The goal of the Community College System's advanced manufacturing initiative is a resilient and robust manufacturing sector fueled by a highly skilled workforce, enabling the state to remain globally competitive as the manufacturing industry – a part of New Hampshire's proud heritage – evolves through innovation.

The community colleges also host the WorkReady NH program, helping job seekers by providing assessment, skill-building and national certification in key workplace skill areas. An initiative supported by the governor and other state economic development leaders, WorkReady NH helps individuals and businesses by strengthening the overall skill levels of the New Hampshire workforce.

From the classroom to the community, New Hampshire's strong network of community colleges has become an integral component in the economic and social well-being of the Granite State in the 21st century.

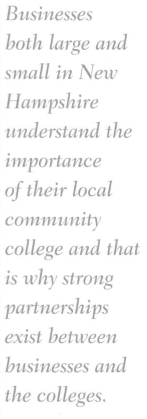

Businesses both large and small in New Hampshire understand the importance of their local community college and that is why strong partnerships exist between businesses and the colleges.

The community colleges offer nearly 200 degree and certificate programs in a wide array of academic and professional fields

New Hampshire Public Television

NHPTV's schedule includes the acclaimed *Saving Songbirds* documentary, a *Windows to the Wild* special with Willem Lange; the popular *Curious George* series; programs that encourage children to explore nature; and the famed documentaries of NH's own filmmaker Ken Burns.

On a summer night more than 50 years ago, New Hampshire Public Television came to life. The program line-up on Channel 11 included shows about public affairs, antiques, sewing, painting and music. What was born that evening in 1959 – a commitment to entertain, educate and enrich the lives of the people in the Granite State – has evolved and grown ever since.

Over the past half century, NHPTV has delivered award-winning PBS and local programming to New Hampshire and northern New England. NHPTV first beamed its programs to TVs as grainy black and white images, then in rich color. With advances in technology, the station's signal has gone from analog to digital, and its reach has extended to multimedia content distributor. Many of NHPTV's programs can now be watched on multiple channels, in high and standard definition, as well as online at nhptv.org.

"I was in first grade when NHPTV first aired," a long-time viewer recalls. "Our teacher let us watch it every day for an hour or so to utilize its educational component. I still watch it for the educational programming as well as the dramas …I've become a well-rounded individual because of NHPTV."

NHPTV's locally focused programs have won numerous accolades, including Boston/New England Emmys, Tellys and New Hampshire Association of Broadcasters awards.

As a member of the PBS network, NHPTV viewers enjoy a range of programs that focus on nature, science, the arts, public affairs, kids and regional topics, on series like *Nature, NOVA, Masterpiece, American Experience, Great Performances, Curious George, Antiques Roadshow, PBS NewsHour*, and the acclaimed documentaries of Ken Burns. Local award-winning favorites like *Windows to the Wild, Roadside Stories, New Hampshire Crossroads* and independently produced programs with a New England focus also are featured in the station's lineup.

"My family loves your [Willem Lange's] adventures on *Windows to the Wild*. After we replicated your hikes on some trails, my sons demanded to see your hiking episodes rather than an episode of Star Wars," a Portsmouth viewer wrote. "That is the best affirmation you will get."

NHPTV is New Hampshire's only statewide, locally owned and operated TV network. Five transmitters carry the station's signal to 98 percent of the Granite State, to more than 1 million viewers each month, and 90,000 children weekly. NHPTV's programs are available free to everyone via over-the-air broadcast, not just through paid cable and satellite companies.

At a time when there's a lack of distinction in what's available on television, NHPTV offers the citizens of the Granite State three unique services: commercial-free, locally focused and PBS TV programs; educational resources (on-air, online and in the community); and a high-tech public safety communications infrastructure.

Because of NHPTV's public service mission, everything it broadcasts and the services it offers are intended to benefit the residents of New Hampshire. Financial support to NHPTV is an investment, not a business transaction. Commercials don't support NHPTV — they can't, by law — its viewers do.

NHPTV's funding comes from viewers, individual donors, corporate underwriters, foundations, and the federal government. This financial support and the power of a large group of enthusiastic volunteers reinforce the value of NHPTV.

"When my family came from Brazil in 1970, everything was so different and exciting," a Manchester viewer noted. "I was 8 years old and Channel 11's programs and *Sesame Street* became part of my schooling. I respect NHPTV as a teacher in my life and many others. Thank you for always being there."

Beyond broadcast, NHPTV offers educational and community initiatives that complement and build on its on-air programs. Many of NHPTV's educational resources and workshops – which are offered to teachers, families and students free of charge – follow state curriculum standards and are used by pre-K through 12th grade students. Teachers can enroll in online PBS TeacherLine courses, a service offering standards-based, graduate-level material. Another online service, PBS LearningMedia, is available to both teachers and families.

Advancing their reading skills through hands-on, active learning, and celebrating the power of creating original illustrated stories, more than 10,000 students in kindergarten through grade 5 have participated in the *NHPTV-PBS Kids Go! Writers Contests* over the years.

"My daughter Holly was not interested in learning to read and write until she decided to enter the contest," wrote a Nashua mother. "Seeing her name and story on your website really excited her. She got out paper and immediately started another story!"

In keeping with its public service focus, NHPTV actively partners with community organizations to spotlight topics such as childhood obesity, bullying, math and science literacy,

The *Windows to the Wild* production crew travels all over New England and beyond to transport viewers to unique natural environments, and offer insight into the history, ecology and special character of each place.

Each year NHPTV sponsors the *PBS Kids Go! Writers Contest,* which encourages creativity and love of reading and writing in grade K – 5 children.

Five transmitters carry the station's signal to 98 percent of the Granite State, to more than 1 million viewers each month, and 90,000 children weekly.

the environment, and aging. Its participation in a national Community Cinema initiative brings PBS Independent Lens documentaries free of charge to cities and towns for screenings and discussions.

And, since its signal reaches all over New Hampshire, NHPTV's state-of-the-art communications network is an integral part of the public safety infrastructure. Its digital datastream and network of transmitter towers are used by state and local police, firefighters and first responders, and municipalities and hospitals to transmit information.

"With many viewing choices on TV and online," said NHPTV President and CEO Peter Frid, "we sometimes are asked, why do we need public broadcasting? And what I say – because this is what I hear so often from our viewers – is that our state and country need a strong public media system with non-partisan news, cultural and educational programs, and one that focuses on local interests. That's why New Hampshire Public Television was created over 50 years ago and why we're still in business today."

Northeast Delta Dental

More than forty-five hundred New Hampshire employers have chosen Northeast Delta Dental to administer their dental benefits.

Account Manager highlights dental benefits offered by subscriber's employer and provides oral health information.

After more than a decade of championing by New Hampshire dentists, the state legislature created the New Hampshire Dental Service Corp., a charitable, not-for-profit organization, in 1961.

In that era, dentists sought a way to provide for the oral health of people around the state by offering dental prepayment programs. The fledgling company was established in Concord, where its headquarters are today, and Wendell E. Fitts, DMD, was elected as its first president in 1966, the year it sold its first group account

Ten years later, Maine Dental Service Corp., based in Saco, and Vermont Dental Service, Inc., based in Burlington, joined New Hampshire Dental Service Corp. in forming a cooperative association called Northeast Delta Dental. At that time, the company had sold 10 group accounts.

Now, 50 years after New Hampshire Dental Service was incorporated, it administers the dental benefits of 750,000 people in Maine, New Hampshire and Vermont. More than 4,500 New Hampshire employers have chosen Northeast Delta Dental to administer their dental benefits and over 170,000 New Hampshire employees and their family members are covered by one of its group dental insurance contracts. Another 5,000 New Hampshire citizens and their families, who do not have access to employer-sponsored dental benefits, are covered by individual contracts.

Group customers include financial institutions, hospitals, school systems, unions, associations and a variety of businesses and nonprofit organizations of all sizes across industry sectors. Because its primary objective is to extend the availability of oral health care, Northeast Delta Dental educates group customers, potential purchasers, subscribers and the public about the value of oral health and offers affordable, high quality dental plans to improve access to dental services.

Passion about its oral health mission drives Northeast Delta Dental's focus on offering service that exceeds the expectations of its customers. It is known throughout northern New England for reinforcing its key promises to customers through a comprehensive service guarantee program, considered a trail blazing initiative in the insurance industry.

"Our Guarantee Of Service Excellence program is great for us and our customers, because it keeps us reevaluating, and improving, every one of our processes," said Thomas Raffio, FLMI, president and CEO since 1995. He introduced the service guarantee program in 1996 in response to customer feedback.

Raffio is an incorporator and the chairman of the board of the Granite State Quality Council. Northeast Delta Dental employees provide leadership for the organization and the company hosts many of the Quality Council's events. The New Hampshire quality program is based on the criteria for the Baldrige National Quality Program.

"Ours is a values-driven company that successfully balances financial health and social responsibility," he said. "Our leadership team follows the principles of servant leadership, enabling all employees, customers, participating dentists and other stakeholders to have a delightful experience with Northeast Delta Dental."

Northeast Delta Dental purposefully created a corporate environment built upon high trust and mutual respect, which has earned it many awards and certifications for its employee-friendly policies.

Through biennial employee surveys, the company finds that its employees love their work and their work environment.

"People like each other here and care about each other and the camaraderie is evident," observes one employee. "The longevity of our employees speaks to this. I still look forward to coming to work every day after 30 years. This is my second home."

Northeast Delta Dental employees set a remarkable standard for volunteering and giving back to their communities. Many of its 184 employees, including six from Maine and four from Vermont, provide leadership to the boards and advisory committees of nonprofit organizations. Many volunteer their time and expertise in other ways.

Northeast Delta Dental has two programs aimed at encouraging its employees to volunteer and invest time in the communities where they live, providing grants to the organizations where employees volunteer and giving them one day off annually for their volunteer work.

In 1995, Northeast Delta Dental incorporated the Northeast Delta Dental Foundation, which awards about $350,000 annually to oral health programs in Maine, New Hampshire and Vermont. Recipients include nonprofit dental clinics and community- and school-based programs that provide oral health education and dental services to people who would not otherwise be reached.

Northeast Delta Dental is noted for its partnerships with other organizations to find lasting oral health solutions and its dedication in encouraging people to view oral health as a vital component of overall health. To that end, the company convenes forums to encourage physicians and dentists to find ways to work together to benefit their patients.

With a half century of experience developing innovative programs for dental benefits administration, Northeast Delta Dental has earned its reputation as an expert in the dental insurance industry.

Northeast Delta Dental continues to listen to its customers and, in response to their suggestions, the company in 2009 launched a comprehensive vision insurance program. DeltaVision° is now offered to Maine and New Hampshire group customers as another employee benefit.

Through its holding company, Northeast Delta Dental acquired a general insurance agency with which it has had a 30-year relationship, enabling the company to offer complementary employee benefits.

Northeast Delta Dental is affiliated with Delta Dental Plans Association, America's largest and most trusted dental benefits carrier. With a network of 39 independent member companies in all 50 states, the District of Columbia and Puerto Rico, it shares a mission to improve the oral health of the nation by making dental care available and affordable to the public through the expansion of dental benefits programs.

"Ours is a values-driven company that successfully balances financial health and social responsibility."

Aerial view of Northeast Delta Dental corporate headquarters, One Delta Drive, Concord, New Hampshire.

Department of Resources & Economic Development

New Hampshire's natural and economic treasures are overseen by the Department of Resources & Economic Development

New Hampshire's quintessential New England Villages, like Washington (above), draw visitors from around the world, they are often home to high tech industries, too.

The diverse New Hampshire landscape, from its scenic shoreline to the rugged North Country, captivates vacationers as well as those who stay, make their homes and establish their businesses in the Granite State.

These natural and economic treasures are overseen by the Department of Resources & Economic Development and its four divisions: Travel and Tourism Development; Parks and Recreation; Forest and Lands, and Economic Development. Together, the agencies are the guardians of the facets of New Hampshire that make its geography, culture and communities so unique.

Each year, New Hampshire welcomes nearly 34 million visitors who come to see its spectacular scenery, outstanding recreation, historic sites and wealth of cultural offerings, as well as a wide array of dining, lodging, cultural and entertainment options.

The Division of Travel and Tourism Development is the steward of the New Hampshire tourism brand. It works to shape and promote the state's image to attract visitors from all over the world, through domestic and international advertising, public relations and its website (visitnh.gov), which all showcase New Hampshire's unique tourism offerings.

Partnering with the seven tourism regions, the DTTD works with officials from the Seacoast, Lakes Region, Merrimack Valley, Monadnock Region, Dartmouth-Lake Sunapee Region, White Mountains and Great North Woods to help them increase the number of vacationers and generate travel and visitor expenditures, which boost the local economy and employment.

DTTD oversees grant administration and coordinates research to monitor and measure the impact of travel and tourism to the state and, through the Bureau of Visitor Services, manages the state's 13 Welcome and Information Centers that provide information to travelers.

New Hampshire's State Parks include some of the Granite State's signature attractions. The Division of Parks and Recreation (www.nhstateparks.org) is the steward of 92 state-owned properties, including Franconia Notch State Park, home of the Flume Gorge, Cannon Mountain Aerial Tramway and former site of the Old Man of the Mountain granite profile; Hampton Beach State Park and four other beaches along the Atlantic Ocean; the birthplace of Daniel Webster; and Mount Washington State Park, on the summit of the Northeast's highest peak.

In all, there are 38 state-owned day-use parks; 19 campgrounds; 17 recreational rail trails; 16 historic sites; 13 natural

Carlisle Wide Plank Floors.
New Hampshire's forests provide recreation, wildlife habitat, open space and the raw material for the wood products industry, which ships New Hampshire-made products worldwide.

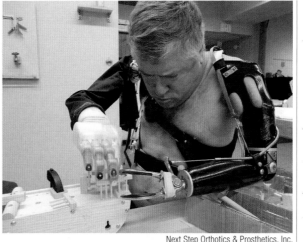

Next Step Orthotics & Prosthetics, Inc.
Chuck Hildreth tests a new robotic arm developed with DARPA funding by New Hampshire inventor Dean Kamen's Manchester-based DEKA Integrated Solutions Corp. in partnership with its Millyard neighbor, Next Step Orthotics & Prosthetics, Inc. Dubbed "The Luke Arm," the prosthetic arm restores functionality to people with upper extremity amputations.

Often, those who first visit the state as tourists, or while at school, college or summer camp, return to live and work here, drawn by the exceptional quality of life.

areas and waysides and Cannon Mountain, the only ski area operated by the state.

The agency is comprised of four bureaus: The Bureau of Park Operations, which oversees state parks, campgrounds, waysides, and natural areas; the Bureau of Trails, which manages motorized trails for snowmobiling and ATV use, as well as non-motorized trails for hiking, biking, cross country skiing, sled dog mushing and equestrian use; the Bureau of Historic Sites, which manages historic properties and other historic resources under stewardship of the Department of Resources and Economic Development; and Cannon Mountain ski area. Together, these bureaus work to protect and preserve these unusual scenic, historical, recreational and natural areas, keeping them accessible to the public.

Forests cover nearly 84 percent of New Hampshire, making it the second-most forested state in the nation, and more than three-quarters of this land is privately owned. Thanks to this rich resource, New Hampshire has a vibrant forest products industry that blends forest-based manufacturing, - recreation and tourism, as well as the Christmas tree and maple syrup industries. The economic value of these components is nearly 4 percent of the Gross State Product.

The Division of Forests and Lands (www.nhdfl.org) protects and promotes the values provided by trees, woodlands and natural communities and is responsible for the management on 167,000 acres of state-owned land. It also enforces state forestry laws and monitors conditions to protect the woods from damaging insects, diseases and wildfires.

Forest and Lands manages the New Hampshire State Forest Nursery, which provides tree and shrub planting stock to landowners and residents for forest plantings and other conservation purposes. Established in 1911, the nursery is the only one of its kind in New England and has provided more than 75 million seedlings.

Often, those who first visit the state as tourists, or while at school, college or summer camp, return to live and work here, drawn by the exceptional quality of life. New Hampshire has been named the Most Livable State in the U.S. several times in the past decade, owing to its low crime rate, quality health care, excellent schools, affordable housing, open space and cultural opportunities. It boasts low taxes; a stable and well-educated workforce; close proximity to the Boston metro market, southern New England, New York and southeast Canada, and a business-friendly state government.

Charged with the responsibility for assisting businesses, the Division of Economic Development (www.nheconomy.com) acts as a single point of contact for businesses at all stages in their growth cycle. The agency prides in its capacity for innovation. It doesn't do "business as usual." Instead, it takes a "no bull" approach, creating innovative programs and services that support established businesses and those considering relocating or expanding to the state.

These programs and services are available at no cost and in addition to providing assistance across a broad spectrum of areas ranging from licensing and financing to permitting and workforce training, the Division of Economic Development works with federal, regional, local and other state agencies, as well as with private sector partners, to deliver a comprehensive array of services.

New Hampshire offers many incentives to businesses that locate here, including business and technical assistance for manufacturers; technical assistance to those companies interested in procuring federal and state contracts and customized reports and personal tours of available office and industrial real estate.

This division also works with New Hampshire businesses to enter and be successful in the international marketplace. The agency plans, develops and administers programs for international trade promotion and foreign market development and coordinates with other public and private organizations involved in concurrent efforts.

New Hampshire Charitable Foundation

Girls find comfort and camaraderie while sharing ideas during circle time at Girls Incorporated of New Hampshire.

Cheryl Senter

The New Hampshire Charitable Foundation funds more than 1,500 organizations annually that make a difference in people's lives, from soup kitchens to the arts.

The Granite State's unique bridge between generous citizens and organizations that can change lives is the New Hampshire Charitable Foundation.

For half a century, the foundation has managed a growing collection of philanthropic funds established by individuals, families and businesses. As the largest private charitable funding source in the state, the foundation makes grants to 1,500 nonprofit organizations annually, from the arts to environmental protection, soup kitchens to youth development.

"We are all united by one common bond, a passion for place: A town, a city, a region, state," said foundation President and CEO Richard Ober. "A community, no matter how you define it."

A community foundation provides a way for local donors to take an organized approach to giving and to better understand the needs in their region. Of the more than 700 community foundations nationwide, the New Hampshire Charitable Foundation is among the oldest and largest. Its student aid program is the largest nongovernmental source of schol-

arships for New Hampshire students. The foundation also has what is arguably the largest governance structure, which includes about 100 volunteer advisory board members around the state. Such breadth and depth of connections make the foundation an organization that knows the ground, knows its communities.

In 2010, the foundation made over 4,300 awards, totaling more than $30 million, to nonprofits and students. The foundation also leveraged its grant making by helping to bring in more than $28 million from outside New Hampshire to support initiatives in clean energy, lead paint poisoning prevention, justice reinvestment and substance use disorder prevention and treatment.

One example of the foundation's work is evident in its Neil and Louise Tillotson Fund, named for the late couple who wanted to provide a means to support the communities of their beloved North Country. Established in 2006, the fund set a daring challenge: Help the North Country move from decades of decline to a vibrant and sustainable economy.

In the past 10 years, Coös County has lost most of its manufacturing base, including furniture making and pulp and paper mills, leaving close to 1,000 residents without good paying jobs that have sustained the region for generations. The Neil and Louise Tillotson Fund provided support to strengthen and build critical community capacity – resilient institutions and collaborative leadership – and to encourage a regional mindset. Berlin City Planner Pamela LaFlamme said the fund has been inspirational, bringing leaders together from across the region for networking and professional development.

"Coös County has a much stronger resource network than we've ever had before," said LaFlamme, one of the 10 members of the fund's advisory committee. "People have realized that they can be proactive in their own destiny. "That's something that has bubbled up here during the last couple of years. Destiny doesn't have to be something that happens to you. You can be part of making sure something good comes of it."

On preparing for the future, Ober notes that the foundation is facing new challenges with the troubled economy. Philanthropy must step up, he said, but no one can expect the charities and churches to pick up all the slack.

"We can't replace cuts in public funding and we shouldn't try," he said. "But we can and must innovate and collaborate better. We need to test, learn, adapt more quickly, find brilliant ideas and bring them to scale. We need to help nonprofits and those they serve to advocate for critical needs - to have a more effective voice in their communities, with policy makers, in the media."

The foundation believes in the importance of independent information and civic dialogue. To that end, it funds independent think tanks, such as the New Hampshire Center for Public Policy Studies and the Carsey Institute, and 21st century town squares including the Forum on New Hampshire's

John Hession

Richard Ober, president and CEO of New Hampshire Charitable Foundation

Future, New Hampshire Listens and New Hampshire Public Radio. It amplifies the voice and capacity of nonprofits by supporting The New Hampshire Center for Nonprofits.

In partnership with government, the foundation can shed more light on important public issues. It can convene leaders from nonprofits, public agencies and business to leverage resources and increase efficiency to help as many people as possible.

"We can make the difference between a life forgotten and a life fulfilled," Ober said. "It's not about charity, and it's not about 'filling gaps'. It's about building stronger and more resilient communities where residents have better access to basic needs, environmental and historic assets are conserved, arts and cultural groups celebrate creativity and diverse perspectives, economic opportunity is available to all, residents stay connected to their neighbors, informed and engaged in civic life. And it's about long-term vision and hope in a short-term world."

A.J. Wolfe, *Concord Monitor*

> *"We can make the difference between a life forgotten and a life fulfilled,"* Ober said.

The foundation supports civic dialogue. Steve Bridgewater asks questions at a Warner town meeting.

The University System of New Hampshire

Thompson Hall, University of New Hampshire

The University System of New Hampshire (USNH) is the state's primary supplier of highly educated citizens and workers. Its four institutions - the University of New Hampshire in Durham and Manchester, Plymouth State University, Keene State College, and Granite State College —annually enroll more than 31,000 students, award more than half of the state's bachelor's degrees and 60 percent of degrees in shortage areas such as engineering, math, information technology, and biological and physical sciences.

Education is the key to New Hampshire's long-term welfare, economic prosperity, and quality of life. More than ever, the potential for each person to succeed and prosper is deter-

mined by his or her ability to think, reason, and participate fully in all facets of life. Providing these critical educational programs and services through teaching, research, and public service is at the heart of the USNH mission.

"Our core values drive what we do," said Edward MacKay, chancellor of the University System. "These include being truly student-centered and committed to affordable access, quality in teaching and research, and engagement by faculty, students and staff in our internal and external communities."

USNH's three residential institutions continually attract a significant number of students from other states and abroad, who help create vibrant learning communities. They are among only 311 US institutions receiving the Community Engagement Classification by The Carnegie Foundation for the Advancement of Teaching. The classification recognizes demonstrated commitment to community partnerships, educational outreach, and service learning.

The University of New Hampshire is a vibrant place: A land-sea-and space-grant university where undergraduate and graduate students engage in daily discovery and the intellectual excitement of doing research with their faculty mentors.

New Hampshire's community-engaged public research university enrolls nearly 17,000 students at its residential campus in Durham and urban campus in Manchester. Recognized as a rising star among research universities, UNH retains the atmosphere of a New England liberal arts college, with a faculty dedicated to undergraduate teaching and research.

Its commitment to engagement and public service serves not only the Granite State, through its many outreach offices such as Cooperative Extension, but nationally and internationally through its public policy expertise in areas as diverse as crimes against children, ocean fisheries management, and rural poverty.

In 2010, the Franklin Pierce Law Center became the University of New Hampshire School of Law. Located in Concord, New Hampshire's only law school is an intimate, innovative institution that is committed to developing students who enjoy challenging dialogue from the first moments of orientation, and grow through the collegiality of a 14:1 student/faculty ratio. In 2011, the UNH School of Law rose to fourth in the specialty rankings for intellectual property law by *U.S. News & World Report*, It was also recognized as a "top tier" school in the overall rankings.

Plymouth State University is a regional comprehensive university with an established reputation for high academic standards. PSU offers bachelor's degrees in more than 45 majors and 60 minors, and master's degrees in more than 70 concentrations in a rich, student-focused learning environment for its nearly 6,000 undergraduate and graduate students. PSU also offers a Certificate of Advanced Graduate Studies and a Doctor of Education in Learning, Leadership, and Community.

The PSU motto is Ut Prosim (That I may serve) and students, faculty, and staff engage communities on a local, regional, national, and international scale in ways that are relevant and practical, as well as mutually beneficial. In each of these roles, PSU has a special commitment of service to the North Country and Lakes Region of New Hampshire.

Keene State College is New Hampshire's public liberal arts college, offering majors in the arts and sciences, professional programs, and selected graduate degrees. Founded in 1909, KSC is one of the most preeminent public liberal arts colleges in the nation. With more than 40 programs of study, including a new nursing program and the nation's only baccalaureate degree program in Holocaust and Genocide Studies, KSC prepares students to think critically, act creatively, and serve the greater good. For its 5,700 students, the college provides rigorous academic programs and a tradition of small classes, faculty-student collaborative research, and service learning.

KSC is a leader in applying the principles of a liberal arts

Aerial view of Plymouth State University and Rounds Hall

Alumni Hall, Keene State College

education to today's challenges. Innovative curriculum focuses on high-impact practices that have earned national praise. The *Princeton Review* has consistently listed Keene State as one of the 218 best colleges in the Northeast and as a top Green College; *U.S. News & World Report* ranks it as one of the top schools in the North.

Granite State College is New Hampshire's public college for students of all ages. Since 1972, GSC has provided statewide access to higher education to more than 54,000 students, both online and at nine campuses statewide. To meet the needs of employers and working adults, the college offers flexible bachelor's and associate's degrees, as well as post-baccalaureate teacher certification programs. In 2011, GSC added its first-ever Master's program, offering an MS degree in Project Management.

Known for its small classes, affordable tuition and supportive faculty, GSC has taken a leading role in providing innovative online degree programs. Ultimately, GSC addresses the needs of New Hampshire's workforce through its practical, relevant and accessible degree programs.

The Derryfield School

Derryfield Middle School students investigate the acoustics of playing outside during their instrumental music class.

Derryfield holds six core values in high esteem: Aim High, Balance, Character, Community, Families, and Individuality, all of which are reflected in the school's culture and programs.

The Derryfield School is a leading independent school for students in grades 6-12, located in Manchester. The mission of the school is to inspire bright, motivated young people to be their best and provide them with the skills and experiences needed to be valued, dynamic, confident, and purposeful members of any community. Derryfield holds six core values in high esteem: Aim High, Balance, Character, Community, Families, and Individuality, all of which are reflected in the school's culture and programs.

Derryfield was founded in 1964 by 39 visionary families in the greater Manchester community who saw a need for a coeducational day school designed to offer an outstanding, traditional coeducational college preparatory education to students living at home. A talented, dedicated and caring faculty, a rigorous academic program, small classes, and rich opportunities in visual and performing arts, athletics and extracurricular activities, were designed to promote intellectual, personal and ethical development, and a lifetime commitment to community.

In September 1965, 102 students in grades 7-10 launched Derryfield's first academic year meeting in leased quarters in downtown Manchester, with grades 11 and 12 added in the two successive years. In March 1967, Derryfield moved to its present campus and celebrated its first commencement in 1968. Enrollment, curricula and co-curricular programs, and the physical facility grew as the school developed its identity, expanded its outreach into area communities, and developed pride in the increasingly demanding academic program. Derryfield's momentum continued in the 1990s with the acquisition of 72 adjacent acres and the addition of a sixth grade. Today, as the school approaches its 50th Anniversary with an enrollment of 368, Derryfield has developed into an educational leader in New Hampshire.

Derryfield's academic facilities include classroom buildings with five fully equipped science laboratories; a technology center with workstations and laptops; a 95-seat multimedia lyceum; a 17,000-volume library with a large subscription database; two art studios; an art gallery; and a 400-seat performing arts center. Outdoor classroom facilities include several miles of cross-country trails, high and low ropes courses, and many acres of woods. A turf field, a full-sized gymnasium, weight-training area, and trainer's room are also valuable learning sites for courses in physical education and health and wellness. In addition, the school opened the new 8,000-square-foot Gateway Building in 2011, which houses administrative offices, the Breakthrough Manchester Program and two additional teaching spaces.

Derryfield's core college-preparatory curriculum is enhanced by more than 70 elective classes and independent learning opportunities. Students entering in the middle school participate in a curriculum that provides a firm background in skills and basic discipline areas. Derryfield's challenging academic program combines a seriousness of purpose with a sense of fun, while the School's inclusive community emphasizes respect, integrity, and kindness. Derryfield students engage the world around them. In their service learning project, geography students explore world cultures by interviewing recent immigrants in a university-sponsored program for English language learners. They research countries of origin and prepare projects on immigrants' individual journeys to America.

As students enter the Upper School, Derryfield's broad, deep, and rigorous curriculum offers a number of AP courses that enable high-achieving students to earn college credit. The academic aspirations of Derryfield students are fully supported by teachers who are energized by seeing students reach their potential. The school's arts environment is both safe and challenging, helping students to gain the self-confidence and skills to grow to their fullest potential as artists and individuals. Pursuing individual interests and potential career paths is at the heart of the Independent Senior Project, a special experiential learning opportunity for seniors. Among other ventures, Derryfield students have served as apprentices to master carpenters, fulfilled internships at architecture, law and investment firms, and volunteered in local hospitals and in orphanages as far away as Nicaragua and Bolivia.

Derryfield is a member of the New Hampshire Interscholastic Athletic Association, participating in Division I, III and IV, according to sport and regularly earns state championships in multiple sports. Derryfield currently has the most athletic offerings of any Division IV school in New Hampshire and has garnered more than 25 state championships in the last 10 years. Supportive of students of all abilities, Derryfield coaches have the passion, expertise and professionalism to coach students who go on to play at the highest levels. Those students who do not participate in interscholastic sports can fulfill their athletics requirement through noncompetitive activities.

The Derryfield community is committed to purposeful involvement in the world outside the school in both the local and global community. In recent years, the reach of the school's service program has expanded to a global scale, with students traveling the globe to volunteer with organizations as widespread as Nepal, the Dominican Republic and Romania.

Closer to home, Derryfield shows its commitment to the local community by serving as the home of Breakthrough Manchester, a tuition-free, year-round, multi-year, academic program serving a diverse community of learners. Breakthrough Manchester is based upon a dual mission of helping promising Manchester Middle School students, particularly those with limited opportunities, build the skills and confidence to enter and succeed in college preparatory high school programs and, through its "students teaching students" model, inspiring talented high school and college students to pursue careers in education. Founded in 1991 at Derryfield, Breakthrough Manchester was the third program to be established in the national Breakthrough Collaborative. Each year, approximately 30 to 35 Derryfield students and alumni serve as teachers in the program. Since its inception, the program has helped over 500 Manchester youth get on the college track and mentored 800 young teachers.

Derryfield's small classes, academic depth and breadth, safe community, and talented faculty combine to foster success in students who want to be their best. Guided by college counselors whose mission is to help students find the school that is the right fit for them, Derryfield students go to some of the top schools in the country. Derryfield students have 100 percent acceptance to four-year colleges but, most important, Derryfield students are 100 percent ready for the world ahead.

Derryfield's small classes, academic depth and breadth, safe community, and talented faculty combine to foster success in students who want to be their best.

The Derryfield girls' varsity soccer team celebrates winning the Division IV State Championships in 2010.

New Hampshire College & University Council

The NHCUC, founded in 1966, is a unique higher education consortium with a diverse membership of public and private, four year and two year colleges and universities.

With over 75,000 students attending New Hampshire's public and private colleges and universities, tomorrow's highly skilled workers and engaged citizens are being educated right here in the Granite State. Recognizing the benefits of working together, New Hampshire's non-profit higher education institutions understand that they benefit from sharing scarce resources and partnering with each other through the New Hampshire College & University Council.

The NHCUC, founded in 1966, is a unique higher education consortium with a diverse membership of public and private, four year and two year colleges and universities. For over 45 years, the NHCUC has worked to provide services and programs that benefit students, faculty, administrators and its member institutions. Through shared library services, collaborative admissions programs, faculty and professional development offerings, and career services the NHCUC connects its member campuses in a variety of effective and important ways.

Recognizing that education does not just occur in the classroom, the NHCUC continuously seeks dynamic partnerships with k-12 schools, businesses and other non-profit organizations. As a co-founder of the New Hampshire Forum on the Future, the NHCUC ensures that the emerging issues and opportunities confronting New Hampshire are regularly addressed at a series of engaged breakfast briefings targeted to the state's key thought leaders. To prepare high school students for college level courses, the NHCUC is the sponsor of the New Hampshire Scholars Program, which partners with local high schools to encourage students to take rigorous academic classes. Recognizing that too often, under-represented student populations are not being well served, the NHCUC administers a statewide Diversity Initiative to encourage minority and other students to explore

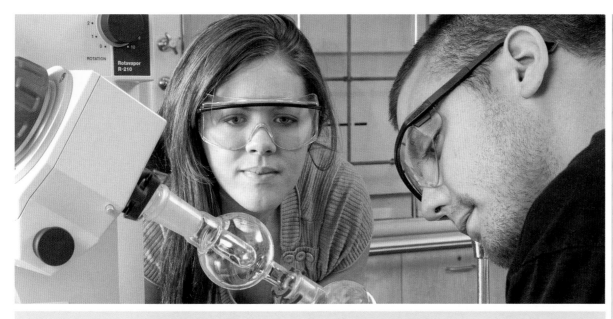

NHCUC Member Institutions

Antioch University New England
www. antiochne.edu

Chester College of New England
www.chestercollege.edu

Colby-Sawyer College
www.colby-sawyer.edu

Community College System of New Hampshire
www.ccsnh.edu

Dartmouth College
www.dartmouth.edu

Franklin Pierce University
www.franklinpierce.edu

Granite State College
www.granite.edu

Hellenic American University
www.hauniv.us

Keene State College
www.keene.edu

MA College of Pharmacy & Health Sciences – Manchester
www.mcphs.edu/manchester

New England College
www.nec.edu

New Hampshire Institute of Art
www.nhia.edu

Plymouth State University
www.plymouth.edu

Rivier College
www.rivier.edu

Saint Anselm College
www.anselm.edu

Southern New Hampshire University
www.snhu.edu

University of New Hampshire
www.unh.edu

higher education opportunities.

New Hampshire's postsecondary education sector represents a major component of the state's economy. Contributing over $4.9 billion annually to New Hampshire's economic engine, colleges and universities provide over 28,000 direct and indirect jobs to the state's labor force, expend over $1 billion on wages and salaries and confer more than 16,000 degrees annually.

Campus Compact for New Hampshire, a partner consortium dedicated to promoting service and service learning opportunities for students and faculty, estimates that New Hampshire's college and university students contribute more than 4.7 million hours to community service each year.

Under the dedicated guidance and leadership of the presidents from each of the NHCUC's member institutions, who serve on the organization's board of directors, the NHCUC is an important convener, advocate, and representative for New Hampshire's diverse array of postsecondary educational institutions. With a world renowned Ivy League institution, strong public university and community college system institutions and a diverse number of private colleges and universities, New Hampshire students can easily find the right institution here in the Granite State.

Thanks to the continued support and active engagement of its member institutions, the NHCUC will continue to play a crucial role in the future of New Hampshire.

Harvard Pilgrim Health Care of New England

Brenda Pizzo

Left to Right: Sue Tenney, Rich Kumpu, Todd Fitzgerald, Beth Roberts, Hugh Rooney, Amy Stuart, Scott Collins, Jim Tollner

Grounded in the mission to improve the quality and value of health care for the people and communities served, Harvard Pilgrim provides a variety of benefit options and funding arrangements designed to meet the needs of New Hampshire employer customers and their employees. The health plan also furnishes its members with well-being programs and advice to help them find their own path to better health.

Harvard Pilgrim's coverage solutions offer strong value and flexibility, supported by the strength of outstanding service performance and relationships with members and customers. Harvard Pilgrim's product line includes:

• Consumer-directed plans with health savings accounts, health reimbursement arrangements, flexible spending account and wellness incentive program options; network-based plans such as ChoiceNet;

• National plan solutions featuring a coast-to-coast network for customers with employees across the country; and

• Retiree coverage solutions for individuals and groups.

Harvard Pilgrim is accepted by doctors and hospitals across New Hampshire, Maine, Massachusetts and beyond. Members can choose to receive care from providers in many different settings, including local private practices, group practices, community health centers and multi-specialty health centers.

Harvard Pilgrim also continues to grow membership through a strategic alliance with UnitedHealth Group. Providing outstanding coverage, service and value for customers with employees across the country, the Passport Connect Program and the Compass Program offer PPO plans with a seamless, nationwide network of more than 500,000 doctors and more than 4,600 hospitals.

The tremendous growth Harvard Pilgrim has experienced in self-funded plans is due largely to the exceptional expertise of Health Plans, Inc., a subsidiary of Harvard Pilgrim. A leading administrator of self-insured plans in the region, Health Plans, Inc. offers to self-funding clients a powerful advantage with flexible, customized plan designs and state-of-the art reporting systems.

For more than 30 years, the Harvard Pilgrim Health Care Foundation has supported leaders and organizations that connect people and communities to care and information. The Foundation does this through the generous giving and volunteerism of its employees, community grants and sponsorships and training for health care professionals. In 2007, the Foundation and Harvard Pilgrim launched Growing Up Healthy, a five-year leadership and funding initiative with the goal of preventing childhood obesity in New Hampshire, Massachusetts and Maine.

The Mount Washington Hotel, opened in 1902, was the site of Bretton Woods Monetary Conference at the end of World War II, where delegates established the World Bank and the International Monetary Fund.

New Horizons for New Hampshire

At the heart of New Horizons are the staff and volunteers dedicated to helping anyone who comes to the door.

Photos: Matthew Lomanno

Charlie Sherman, Executive Director

Every day is a new day at New Horizons for New Hampshire for people in need of food, shelter and supportive services.

These are the services first provided out of a borrowed Winnebago in 1979 and since then, New Horizons has evolved into one of the leading advocates for those who are living with hunger and homelessness in the state, serving 70,000 meals annually and providing countless people with the help they need to make a fresh start.

The nonprofit operates two emergency shelters, a food pantry and soup kitchen, and provides access to medical and mental health care services. About 60 percent of those who come in for a clean bed, shower, meals and supportive services are from Manchester, with the balance coming from all over the state.

"New Horizons confronts the grittiest of issues of our time with a commitment to meet each client's needs," said Richard Ober, president of the New Hampshire Charitable Foundation.

Homelessness is not new and it has not changed much over the years - people fall on hard times and need to reach out for a helping hand to survive. It is a year-round struggle that is not easy.

New Horizons sees that in its statistics. The organization serves an average of 800 children and their families each month, providing meals and groceries. The main dormitory shelter accommodates an average of 72 people per night, while Angie's Shelter for Women is a 16-bed facility where women receive support and education on how to cope with the challenges that brought them there.

More than shelter and food, New Horizons also provides case management, on-site recovery meetings and medical services, which are provided through a partnership with Catholic Medical Center's Healthcare for the Homeless project. Both New Horizons and Angie's clients also have access to mental health services through The Mental Health Center of Greater Manchester.

An alumni program invites former clients back to New Horizons to offer help and mentoring.

At the heart of New Horizons are the staff and volunteers dedicated to helping anyone who comes to the door.

"I am proud that there are so many hard working organizations such as New Horizons all across our great state helping to meet the needs of some of our most vulnerable citizens," said Gov. John H. Lynch. "New Horizon's good work is truly making a difference in many people's lives."

The Flume Gorge, in Franconia Notch State Park, draws thousands of visitors each year who come to see the soaring granite walls and rushing waters of one of New Hampshire's most popular attractions.

New Hampshire Public Radio

Over 17,000 listeners contribute to the station annually, as do more than 400 local companies.

NHPR's new broadcast center on Pillsbury Street in Concord.

Joseph St. Pierre

I n 1981, tucked away at the far left end of the radio dial, sat the country's newest public radio station. At that time, the programming on 89.1 was scant – a mere four hours per day – and if listeners ventured too far outside of the Capital region, the signal went from static to silence.

From those humble beginnings grew one of the nation's most successful non-commercial broadcast services. Affectionately known as 'WEVO' in the early years, New Hampshire Public Radio kept its eyes on the prize – fulfilling its mandate to become New Hampshire's trusted source for balanced, in-depth news, information and analysis. Today, NHPR reaches all corners of the state, with 13 stations from Nashua to Colebrook, from Portsmouth to the Upper Valley. Located in a state-of-the-art broadcast center in Concord, NHPR offers a unique mix of local, national and international news and serves about approximately 173,000 listeners each week and thousands more online.

"Over the years, our core mission hasn't changed," said Betsy Gardella, president and CEO of NHPR, "but the quality of the programming, the depth and breadth of our newsroom, and the reach of our service has made us an essential source for thousands of listeners. While radio is core to our business, we've become a 'multi-platform' media company offering digital streams, iPhone Apps, podcasts, Facebook pages and Twit-

ter feeds. It's a new world filled with opportunities to reach more and more people in real time."

The mission of NHPR is to create a more informed public, one challenged and enriched by a deeper understanding and appreciation of state, national and worldwide events, ideas and culture. New Hampshire is a state where every citizen has a say in both local and state government, so the station is committed to providing news and information that helps people participate in civic life and make informed decisions.

NHPR's flagship program, *The Exchange*, is a daily public affairs call-in program. For 15 years, Laura Knoy, a former NPR newscaster with New Hampshire roots, has hosted the show. *The Exchange* focuses primarily on politics, government, the economy, environment and education, and has become an essential stop for presidential hopefuls throughout the New Hampshire Primary season.

At noon, listeners across the Granite State tune in to *Word of Mouth*, a magazine show about arts and ideas. Host Virginia Prescott interviews musicians, writers, scientists, humorists, inventors, and even the occasional robot, to reveal innovative trends that will undoubtedly shape our future. *The Folk Show*, a long-standing New Hampshire tradition, boasts a loyal audience of folk lovers who tune in each Sunday night for folk tunes, live performances and artist interviews. NHPR also produces a weekly environment feature about New

Hampshire's flora and fauna, *Something Wild*, as well as the weekly *Giving Matters*, which spotlights New Hampshire's nonprofit sector and the important role that philanthropy plays in the state.

In the tradition of public radio, NHPR counts on its listeners for financial support, and they have demonstrated their appreciation time and again. Over 17,000 listeners contribute to the station annually, as do more than 400 local companies. In 2009, NHPR concluded a $6.5 million capital campaign, enabling the station to construct and outfit new studios, upgrade transmitter sites across the state and install the latest digital equipment. Back-up capacity was improved to ensure uninterrupted transmission, regardless of the weather.

The success of this campaign demonstrated the value of NHPR's service and the loyalty of its audience. In all, 1,800 people contributed gifts ranging from $50 to $1 million.

"Public radio is a big tent," Gardella said, "and everyone is welcome. This service is possible because the community comes together and gives what they can. It is truly a populist medium."

NHPR is proud to be part of the NPR network, broadcasting *Morning Edition*, *All Things Considered* and *Talk of the Nation*. *The World* from PRI and *News* from the BBC provide outstanding international coverage that serves as a perfect complement to NHPR's locally produced New Hampshire news. The station boasts an award-winning newsroom that provides in-depth coverage of business, health, environment, arts, politics and education.

Cultural programs include *Fresh Air* with Terry Gross, *A Prairie Home Companion* with Garrison Keillor, *Studio 360* with Kurt Andersen and *This American Life* with Ira Glass. The entertainment shows *Car Talk* and *Wait, Wait Don't Tell Me* are some of NHPR's most popular programs and the station regularly brings national shows, hosts, journalists and producers to the state in an effort to connect with the community in exciting ways. Recent guests have included Brooke Gladstone and Bob Garfield, co-hosts of *On the Media*; Krista Tippett, host of *On Being*; Carl Kasell, *Wait, Wait Don't Tell Me!*; Diane Rehm; and reporters Jackie Northam, David Folkenflik, and Jamie Tarabay.

With The Music Hall in Portsmouth, NHPR produces *Live @ The Loft*, a series of music performances and musician interviews on stage in live broadcasts and *Writers on a New England Stage*, which has hosted authors including Madeline Albright, John Updike, E.L. Doctorow, Simon Winchester, Joseph Ellis, Elizabeth Gilbert, Joyce Carol Oates, Ann Patchett, Neil Gaiman, David McCullough and many others. There is always something exciting happening at NHPR – on air, online and on stage.

Looking ahead, the station embraces "all things digital," Gardella said.

"To quote Wayne Gretzky: 'You have to skate where the puck is going,'" she said. "We're keenly aware of the changes around us, from tablets to smart phones to connected cars. We intend to be there for future generations, the best content, news, culture and music, where and how they want it. And all the while, we'll stay true to our mission and our radio roots."

"Public radio is a big tent," Gardella said, "and everyone is welcome. This service is possible because the community comes together and gives what they can. It is truly a populist medium."

Brady Carlson

NHPR's Laura Knoy (second from left) talks with three New Hampshire booksellers: Dan Chartrand of Water Street Bookstore in Exeter (left), Michael Herrman of Gibson's Bookstore in Concord (second from right) and Jeff Smull of Toadstool Bookshop in Keene (right).

PC Connection, Inc.

Yesterday...

Back in the early 1980s, the PC Connection raccoon mascot made his debut in PC magazines everywhere. The raccoon symbolized adaptability, innovativeness, and tenacity—traits that underlie the Company's remarkable success.

When Patricia Gallup and David Hall met on the Appalachian Trail, the concept of personal computing was still an idea slightly off the beaten path. Later, while working together at Hall's family business in New Hampshire, IBM released the IBM-PC—the first personal computer built for business. It wasn't long before the pair of young entrepreneurs set out to make computer technology more accessible for everyday users.

It was the experience of trying to purchase a PC for their employer that gave the pair their first glimpse into the emerging industry of personal computing. The closest computer store was an hour and a half drive away—and they knew this would be true almost everywhere else in America. Realizing that many companies would be unable to keep up with the rapidly burgeoning new PC industry, Gallup and Hall recognized an opportunity to provide customers with the information, products, and support needed to integrate technology into their businesses. In 1982, PC Connection was launched as a direct marketing business specializing exclusively in products developed for the IBM-PC. The goal was to provide the technical knowledge, superior customer service, and affordable pricing to help busy people connect with a revolutionary technology they knew they wanted, but didn't have the expertise to implement on their own.

Tucked away in the quiet, picturesque town of Marlow, NH (population 600), the PC Connection headquarters occupied a former woodworking mill—the beginning of the company's longstanding passion for renovating existing buildings. Using Gallup's savings of $8,000, Gallup and Hall purchased inventory and took out a 1/9th-page ad in *Byte* magazine. Once the magazine reached subscribers, the phone started ringing and it hasn't stopped since.

Answering telephones during the day and packing orders at night, Gallup and Hall worked long hours to ensure customers enjoyed the best possible buying experience. As word of this superior service spread, PC Connection began to expand. In 1984, the company added the MacConnection brand to its services; this division focuses exclusively on products for the Apple Macintosh.

After five years in business, PC Connection was named to the Inc. 500 as the fastest organically growing company in the United States—and the second fastest growing company overall. In the years to come, the company expanded to include an outbound managed account program aimed toward corporations, government, and educational customers. With more than 1,000 employees and sales of over $750 million, the company went public on the NASDAQ exchange under the symbol PCCC in March of 1998.

PC Connection established its reputation as a pioneer in the industry early on and set the standard for the levels of service and support customers expect in the marketplace today. PC Connection became known as an innovator and service leader by introducing toll-free technical support before, during, and after the sale. At a time when purchasers often waited 4–6 weeks for delivery, PC Connection implemented Everything Overnight® shipping for all orders on in-stock product, including custom-configured PCs. Helping customers spend less time on the phone placing orders, the company introduced One-Minute Mail Order®—a revolutionary technology that used Caller ID to fill orders in under one minute through instant electronic access to customer records. PC Connection was constantly on the lookout for services that would differentiate the company from the competition and offer customers a higher level of comfort and convenience. PC Connection's goal has always been to 'wow' the customer—to exceed their expectations in terms of the level of service offered.

In 1998, PC Connection completed its renovation of a former strip-mall in Merrimack, NH, designing a green, state-of-the-art building to serve as the Company's current corporate headquarters. The facility houses a data center and an advanced Customer Briefing Center where customers can attend interactive demonstrations and learn about the latest IT products in a real-world environment.

Today...

PC Connection began in 1982 as a direct "mail-order" supplier of software and peripherals exclusively for the newly released IBM-PC, and continually added new products and innovative services to its portfolio. "PC Connection is a Fortune 1000, publicly held company that provides professional offices; small-and medium-sized businesses; and large enterprise, government, and educational institutions with leading-edge IT solutions and exemplary service," says Patricia Gallup, Co-Founder and Chairman of the Board. The company's knowledgeable experts can assist customers with every aspect of the design, deployment, management, and staffing of their IT initiatives. PC Connection offers a wide variety of solutions—including assessments focused on server, storage, networking, security, and virtualization technologies, as well as on-site managed services and staff augmentation—to ensure customers get the most value and performance out of their IT investments.

Offering more than 300,000 products, a nationwide network of service partners, and teams of certified technical experts, PC Connection continues to expand its capabilities to meet evolving customer needs. From virtualization and cloud computing to mobility and security solutions, the company pushes the boundaries of information technology to provide the performance, value, and efficiency that customers deserve. "Applying a comprehensive approach to IT, with services from inventory planning to asset disposition, PC Connection enables organizations across the country to see beyond their immediate needs and build solutions that deliver maximum return on investment throughout the IT lifecycle," says Timothy McGrath, President and Chief Executive Officer.

Thirty years after its founding, PC Connection has grown its annual sales to nearly $2 billion and employs more than 1,800 workers. The company has appeared on the Fortune 1000 for the last 10 years and has been named to *Forbes* America's Most Trustworthy Companies, *Businessweek* World's Top 100 Technology Companies, and the InformationWeek 500. Deeply rooted in the Granite State values that helped shape the company, PC Connection is committed to historical and environmental conservation. Building upon a rich history of innovation and exemplary service, PC Connection stands poised to enjoy continued success and growth as a trusted IT advisor and supplier. And while information technology has forever changed the way the world lives, works, and plays, PC Connection remains steadfastly dedicated to Gallup's original vision—offering customers a level of service that consistently exceeds their expectations.

"PC Connection is a Fortune 1000, publicly held company that provides professional offices; small- and medium- sized businesses; and large enterprise, government, and educational institutions with leading-edge IT solutions and exemplary service," says Patricia Gallup, Co-Founder and Chairman of the Board.

Above:
Co-Founder and Chairman of the Board Patricia Gallup has appeared on *Fortune* magazine's list of top young entrepreneurs, *CRN*'s Most Powerful Women of the Channel, and *Working Woman*'s list of the Top 50 Women Business owners in the United States.

1982 ■ PC Connection is founded

1987 ■ Named #2 on the Inc. 500

1995 ■ Best Mail Order Company by *PC World* magazine—for the 5th time

1998 ■ PC Connection completes Initial Public offering

■ Patricia Gallup receives the National Entrepreneur of the Year Award for Principle-Centered Leadership

1999 ■ Sales top $1 billion

2000 ■ Ranks #7 on *Businessweek* World's Top 100 Technology Companies

2001 ■ Debut on Fortune 1000

■ Better Business Bureau of New Hampshire—Torch Award for Marketplace Ethics

2002 ■ Appears on *Washington Technology* Big Dogs Top 100 Federal Prime Contractors for Information Technology Services

2006 ■ PC Connection CEO Patricia Gallup is named as one of the Top 50 Executives by *VARBusiness*

2008 ■ *Forbes* America's Most Trustworthy Companies—Highest Ranking

■ Top Supply Chain Innovation and Retail Industry Awards; #8 Overall on 2008 InformationWeek 500

2010 ■ Winner of Operational Excellence Award at Microsoft Worldwide Partner Conference

2011 ■ Celebrates 10th consecutive year on the Fortune 1000

■ Secures spot as one of InformationWeek 500 Top Innovators

Pellettieri Associates, Inc.

An understated landscape provides space for family, entertaining or quiet reflection on the natural beauty of New Hampshire.

eyond the fields, a pond, the orchards and a stand of maple trees, in the yard of the stately old colonial and massive barn, there had once been a view of Mount Kearsage that was now being reclaimed by nature.

The owners of the house, a Boston attorney and a Harvard University professor, planned to retire there and called in landscape architect George Pellettieri, giving him a mission to restore that splendid view as part of a renovation project. The solution - relocating the driveway - preserved the established landscape, framing the home with the orchards, fields and maples for those coming to the house, and when the couple drove away from the house every weekend, a spectacular view of the mountain bid them farewell.

The couple liked the view so much, and seeing what they were leaving every time they drove back to the city, they decided to retire early.

"Our job is helping people do on the outside what architects do for people on the inside," said Pellettieri, founder, president, and owner of Pellettieri Associates Inc. in Warner. "The process for each profession is the same. People use our outdoor spaces, which we organize to be functional, creative, comforting and to meet the needs and desires of our clients. We work from the site selection and design in the beginning, through the final construction and finishing touches in the end."

For Pellettieri, his company's work is based on relationships.

His staff strives to develop relationships with local vendors and suppliers, other businesses and their employees, their clients and the environment. While granite cobbles from China or India might be cheaper, PAI still buys from the local quarries at Swenson Granite. It's important to PAI to keep the jobs in New Hampshire and keep the money in New Hampshire as well.

Pellettieri came to the Granite State in 1976 to work as the landscape architect at the University of New Hampshire, where he got to know people across the state that cared about the environment and worked in the "Green Industry." He left UNH in 1980 and created a partnership with a small landscape contractor, striking out on his own three years later and establishing Pellettieri Associates Inc. In 1985, the company moved to Warner, and by 2011, had grown to 25 employees doing work throughout New England and sometimes across the country. One residential client admired Pellettieri's work so much, he took him and a team to Aspen, Colo. and La Jolla, Calif. to work on his other homes.

Throughout the years, PAI has worked on numerous residential properties, often collaborating with architects on a large number of lakefront homes, old and new.

"New Hampshire is a great state and has an abundance of natural beauty," said Pellettieri, a former member of the Governor's Commission on the Comprehensive Shoreline Protection Act. "We focus our efforts to help maintain that valuable resource. It is inevitable that residents are going to tear down summer cottages and build year-round homes. In helping make the rules and regulations, and also being involved in the design process, at least we can educate clients about the need for shoreline protection and preservation. We strive for more sustainable solutions that help enhance and maintain the experience of being on the water."

Beyond residential projects, PAI has worked on multi-disciplinary teams on commercial, and institutional properties such as the Concord Monitor facility, Phillips Exeter Academy, Holderness School, St. Paul's Church in Concord, as well as numerous parks, cemeteries and recreational projects. Working on Plymouth State University's Lamson Library expansion in the 1990s opened the opportunity to help the school further develop and carry out its master plan. As the campus at Plymouth State expanded, the town also grew, bringing with it several projects by the New Hampshire Department of Transportation, including a bridge and rotary intersection, where PAI lent its expertise to assist the state in planning and enhancing the roadways and bikeways of the community.

The firm, which has earned many awards over the years, balances good design, form and function, sustainability and reasonable development, with protecting the environment. Working closely with the client from start to finish, PAI offers a full range of landscape architectural design services for commercial, public and institutional sites; single- and multi-family residences; site planning and engineering; wetlands and shoreland permitting; major tree evaluations; view management and more.

"On lakeside residential projects, we show clients that they don't have to clear-cut the trees to establish a view," Pellettieri said. "Often by adjusting building orientation, we can improve the views, create a 'framed view' of the lake through the trees

A highly-skilled PAI employee carefully saw-cuts a one of a kind, 14 foot, New Hampshire stone, with no margin for error.

and help them be a "better neighbor" by being less visible from the lake."

Construction services include site development, landscape construction of stone walls, patios, walkways and driveways, drainage systems, fences, site amenities, pools, water features, plantings, fine garden services -- all done with as much local labor and local products as possible.

"We are all connected. The threads of our relationships create the fabric of life, the fabric of our communities, the great state of New Hampshire, and the fabric of what makes us a great nation," Pellettieri said. "There are great people in New Hampshire doing great things."

And Pellettieri Associates Inc. is among them.

While granite cobbles from China or India might be cheaper, PAI still buys from the local quarries at Swenson Granite. It's important to PAI to keep the jobs in New Hampshire and keep the money in New Hampshire as well.

The final grill placement, set in stone and boulders, frames a multi-level patio and water feature in this elegant lakeside landscape

The Inns & Spa at Mill Falls

Church Landing, Meredith Bay

Meredith has undergone a remarkable transformation over the last twenty six years, and The Inns and Spa at Mill Falls have played a major role in that transformation.

In the early 1980s, the lakeside town of Meredith was at a crucial point in its evolution, struggling with how to develop responsibly and revitalize its downtown area without jeopardizing its small town character and charm, historic resources, and environmental assets.

Over the next 30 years, developers of the Inns and Spa at Mill Falls, who had a vision for creating a picturesque town on the shore of Lake Winnipesaukee, changed Meredith from a dilapidated mill town into a world-class resort village.

The transformation began in 1983, when three investors bought an Industrial Revolution-era mill building, which had deteriorated into an unsightly sprawl. The former linen mill was preserved and turned into a four-floor marketplace, along with three new retail buildings. The doors opened for business in 1984 as the Mill Falls Marketplace, followed by the magnificent 54-room Inn at Mill Falls a year later.

Ten years later, in 1993, the owners of the Inns and Marketplace purchased a three-story flat roofed office building, which was built in 1968. It had dominated the lakefront and was surrounded by town parks. After reconstruction and renovation, the 24-room Inn at Bay Point and the Boathouse Grille opened in May 1995, which later became Lago Costa Cucina.

Not long after that, the neighboring Chase's Country Town House, a family-owned restaurant and local landmark dating back to 1949, was up for sale. The Inns obtained the property and turned it into what is now The Chase House Inn and conference center. The Chase House at Mill Falls and CAMP restaurant opened in 1998.

Just a year later, in July of 1999, an unsightly gas station along Route 3 was renovated and reborn into the retro-style of a 1940s country filling station, complete with a clapboard-sided store.

When the St. Charles Catholic parish moved to a new location in 2003, The Inns acquired the old church and the land, arguably one of the most desirable properties on the Meredith waterfront. Rather than raze the church, designers incorporated a stunning Adirondack design into the handsome brick building and in May 2004, Church Landing and the Lakehouse Grille celebrated their grand opening. The world-class Cascade Spa welcomed guests two months later inside Church Landing.

Church Landing will unveil its newest expansion in 2012 with two new lakefront buildings, the Birch and Boathouse Lodges, featuring 13 ultra-chic guestrooms, an indoor/outdoor pool and an outdoor patio.

Remaining true to a vision, Meredith has evolved into a charming, yet vibrant, community.

New Hampshire's woods, silent and serene, are inviting for walks and quiet contemplation.

New Hampshire
High Technology Council

In times of crisis, Global Relief Technologies of Portsmouth puts in the hands of those on the front lines equipment that can provide real-time data collection from the field with its Rapid Data Management System.

The New Hampshire High Technology Council plays a role in the growth and success of the technology sector by focusing on its mission to advance innovation throughout the Granite State.

Technology lives in New Hampshire. The state ranks among the top 10 states in its concentration of jobs in science, technology, engineering and math, which is 11 percent higher than the national average in the United States. In recent years, New Hampshire has had almost twice as many patents per person than the national average.

The New Hampshire High Technology Council plays a role in the growth and success of the technology sector by focusing on its mission to advance innovation throughout the Granite State. Founded in 1983, the council is the voice of technology and innovation, bringing together the private and public sectors to establish and maintain financial, technical, legislative and educational programs that support research and economic development to position New Hampshire as a tech leader in the nation.

The main driver in the technology sector is New Hampshire's competitive advantage. The state has one of the lowest overall tax burdens among the states and is frequently ranked among the top three. Its standard of living has also ranked first or second nationally in the last decade.

It has a highly educated workforce, with more than one-third of the state's residents holding a bachelor's degree or higher, compared to about 27 percent nationally. New Hampshire is one of the most wired states in the country,

P.T. Sullivan

Dyn co-founders Jeremy Hitchcock and Tom Daly have built one of the most influential Internet infrastructure companies in the world, growing to more than 100 employees at their Manchester, NH-based headquarters.

with fiber optic cable reaching most of the state. There is a strong entrepreneurial spirit, with frequent interaction between businesses and higher education communities that supports start-ups and fledgling companies, especially in the tech sector.

This is amplified by local sources of venture and angel capital, including the The New Hampshire Innovation Commercialization Center in Portsmouth, which mentors, funds, develops and spins-off young tech companies.

New Hampshire is ranked year after year as one of the best places to live in the United States for quality of life.

The core of New Hampshire's tech sector is manufacturing, which contributes the highest amount of economic activity to the state's gross state product, approximately 4 percent more than the next highest contributor. About 60 percent of those jobs are in advanced manufacturing, with high standards of operational excellence.

Arc Energy is one of the most cutting-edge manufacturing companies in New Hampshire, providing innovative semiconductor scale technologies, turnkey solutions and expertise for companies to meet the demands of the solid-state lighting and other clean energy markets. Arc Energy's unique c-axis sapphire technology platform enables semiconductor scale manufacturing for the LED industry. Customers around the world use ARC Energy's technology and are in mass production for large diameter sapphire.

The company's turnkey solutions enable new entrants in LED sapphire material manufacturing to ramp up to mass production scale very quickly. Arc Energy's turnkey process and equipment solutions range from growing large diameter sapphire to coring, handling, inspecting and recycling sapphire materials.

Global Relief Technologies in Portsmouth serves humanitarian, government and commercial markets throughout the world with rapid field data collection and real-time analysis and collaboration with its Rapid Data Management System. It is an easy-to-use, innovative, patented business solution enabling users to collect and instantaneously share data in real-time, even in the most extreme environments.

RDMS assessments are collected with GPS coordinates and photographs, which allow field workers to track their efforts within a greater geographical context in the form of GIS mapping, satellite imagery and image assessment, preventing redundancy in efforts and ensuring proper distribution of resources, while allowing for enhanced levels of data analysis.

In addition to data collection and collaboration services, RDMS provides a 24/7 support team that monitors collection efforts by field workers. The team works closely with management to tailor reporting and analysis to the clients' specific needs.

Many New Hampshire technology companies serve worldwide markets.

President Obama visit to Arc Energy.

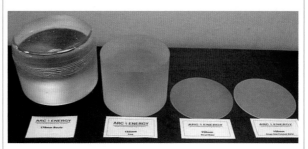

Sapphire for LED manufacturing.

The staff at Portsmouth's PixelMEDIA staff show off the shiny new iPads they received by surprise.

New Hampshire
High Technology Council (Continued)

New Hampshire is a state that has embraced the digital age.

Party time is also the bottom line. Dyn cut the ribbon on a new 24,000 square-foot facility in Manchester's historic Amoskeag mill district in 2011, complete with a full stage for live events. Indie rockers M.T. Bearington, center, played for more than 500 people at Dyn's opening bash.

Many New Hampshire technology companies serve worldwide markets and a prime example is **Dynamic Network Services** of Manchester. Founded in 1998, DYN is the worldwide Internet Infrastructure-as-a-Service leader, powering DNS and email delivery for more than 4 million enterprise, small business and personal users.

With 17 data centers around the world, including London and San Francisco, as well as 100 percent uptime for over 10 years, DYN's commitment to customer relationships and engineering excellence is key to its success. Those business relationships include Fortune 50 companies, as well as start-ups, and nearly everything in between. The company's four key customer vertical markets are advertising and media, e-commerce, software-as-a-service and web 2.0/fast growth.

New Hampshire has a strong software sector, including **AutoDesk** in Manchester, a world leader in 3-D design, engineering and entertainment software. Customers across the manufacturing, architecture, building, construction

Courtesy of Mortenson Construction and RTKL Associates Inc.
Rendering of a hospital showing external architectural features and internal building components. Autodesk(R) Revit(R), Autodesk(R) Navisworks(R), and Autodesk(R) 3ds Max(R) software products were used in the design process. Silver Cross Hospital.

and media and entertainment industries, including 16 Academy Award winners for Best Visual Effects, use AutoDesk software to design, visualize and simulate their

Demonstrating that relationships matter, PixelMEDIA co-founders Erik Dodier and Thomas Obrey hosted their 2011 client appreciation event at historic Fenway Park.

ideas before they are ever built or created, like blockbuster visual effects to buildings that create their own energy to electric cars and batteries that power them.

Through applications for iPhone, iPad and Android, AutoDesk makes design technology accessible to professional designers as well as students, homeowners and casual creators.

New Hampshire has embraced the digital age, largely due to a few pioneering businesses that have successfully navigated this ever changing landscape.

PixelMEDIA of Portsmouth, established in 1994, is one of the classic businesses of the modern age. It is a web design studio that builds clean, usable web sites, combining research, design and technology to help companies achieve better business results, increased revenue and decreased costs. Services include delivering web and mobile solutions, application design and development, user interface design, multimedia design, brand identity, search engine marketing and website hosting and maintenance. PixelMEDIA's customers include industry leaders in technology, financial services, utilities, higher education and consumer products.

With companies like these, the constant challenge is how to generate the educated workforce they need and the New Hampshire High Technology Council has made education its top priority for the past seven years for two reasons.

A projected 64 percent of the new jobs in New Hampshire in the next 10 years will require a post-secondary education and the technology sector will need to hire an increasing number of those graduates to replace retiring Baby Boomers. While the quality of graduates from New Hampshire colleges and universities is high and the number of students pursuing degrees in the physical sciences and engineering is increasing, there aren't enough graduates with engineering, science or technology degrees to meet the growing demand and to replace those who are retiring.

An increasing number of companies are supplementing education in the schools with the in-house training of employees, often using seasoned senior and retired employees to train the younger ones. This kind of scenario is not indigenous to New Hampshire, and is common in other states.

To encourage the Granite State's technology workforce to continue growing and meet the needs of the companies who need skilled workers, the council has created, and supported, several initiatives that improve collaboration between businesses and educators that encourage more high school students to attend college and, once they graduate, to remain in New Hampshire, working for companies that need their expertise.

The New Hampshire State Scholars program, which operates in nearly two-thirds of the state's high schools, is charged with preparing students for college by working with schools to insure curricula is rigorous and relevant and to encourage businesses to mentor students on into college. The New Hampshire High Technology Council is a charter member of the program and its president sits on the board of directors.

As those college students prepare for graduation, the marketing program 'Stay, Work, Play' is aimed at getting the message to them that they can find well-paying jobs here and live the New Hampshire lifestyle. The New Hampshire High Technology Council is a charter member of the group of business and education leaders that developed the program.

To match college students with the internships they need, a member of the council's board of directors created an initiative, and a sophisticated website, to match students with New Hampshire companies offering internships.

Together with secondary and post-secondary educators, the council is a co-convener in the planning of a Business and Education Roundtable, providing support of new initiatives that not only brings education into the 21st century, but meets the needs of students, businesses and the state's economy.

The next generation of science and technology leaders are now in New Hampshire's secondary schools. State test rates show that 65 percent of New Hampshire eighth graders are proficient in math – above the national average and students score above the U.S. average in science.

These are some of the reasons why the technology sector are bullish on New Hampshire's future and work to make certain that education remains one of the state's competitive advantages.

While New Hampshire ranks high nationally for its number of educated citizens, the council realizes that the continuous improvement in the education of citizens is the key to a healthy and prosperous technology sector and to the state's economy.

The technology sector will need to hire an increasing number of those graduates to replace retiring Baby Boomers.

Stonyfield Farm

Gary Hirshberg, CEO of Stonyfield Yogurt

In the early 1980s, Gary Hirshberg and Samuel Kaymen wanted to sell organic, socially responsible yogurt, but they had two problems: No supply and no demand.

Deciding that reality wasn't going to come between them and their plan, the two men continued to work every day out of their leaky barn in Wilton, milking cows and coaxing old farm equipment to fire up.

It would take nine years to turn a profit, but they finally did and together, the two men made Stonyfield Farm the leading organic yogurt maker in the country, putting their special recipe yogurt in grocery stores big and small.

With Hirshberg as the company's 'CE-Yo,' the business has expanded over the past three decades, now employing approximately 425 people in its New Hampshire facility. In 2001, Stonyfield Farm entered into a partnership with Groupe Danone, and in 2005, Hirshberg became managing director of Stonyfield Europe, a joint venture with Danone, which has started organic yogurt brands in Canada, Ireland, and France.

Even with all of its success, the core values of the company have never wavered: Help family farms survive, help the planet, promote and educate the public on the benefits of organic, and to do it all in New Hampshire.

"As a lifelong resident and a third generation New Hampshire manufacturer, I believe that our state is distinctly advantageous for business," Hirshberg said. "It's related to our work ethic and values, our education system, our natural environment, our sense of community, our democratic institutions, and our overall quality of life."

Agriculture and the environment brought the two men together. At the time, Kaymen and his family were running a non-profit agricultural school out of their farm in Wilton. Even then, Kaymen was known as one of the country's early authorities on organic and bio-dynamic agriculture.

Hirshberg was an activist, author, windmill manufacturer and entrepreneur. The two met and Kaymen recruited Hirshberg, who helped map out a business plan for the school and charted a course for Stonyfield Yogurt.

Stonyfield's organic yogurt speeds off the production line

Kaymen, a diabetic, had been experimenting for years to find a recipe for a mild, healthful yogurt with no added sugar. When he discovered one, he started selling it to local health food stores as a way of funding the school in Wilton.

Hirshberg wanted to expand yogurt sales, but more yogurt meant more cows, a barn and building a business, which was a daunting plan for two men. Kaymen and his wife, along with Hirshberg, were the only ones milking the cows, making and delivering the yogurt, not to mention convincing local stores to sell the product.

But it worked.

By 1988, construction got underway for the plant in Londonderry and Stonyfield Farm and its products became staples for healthy-minded consumers. Kaymen retired in 2000, but the vision he and Hirshberg had set out with remains the company's strong foundation.

After perfecting their organic yogurt, they expanded their line of certified organic products to include yogurt drinks, frozen yogurt, ice cream, YoBaby, YoKids, Organic Oikos Greek yogurt, O'Soy cultured soy yogurts and fluid milk.

In the process, Stonyfield has become a bastion of social and environmental responsibility.

The company's 'Profits for the Planet' program gives 10 percent of its annual profits to individuals and organizations working to restore and protect the environment. The company also uses its lids to advocate causes and educate consumers on important issues. Stonyfield has also significantly reduced waste stemming from its plant, which is partially run with the help of a large solar panel array on its roof.

Stonyfield also helps the local community, like hosting a 5k run that benefits Beautify Londonderry, an organization dedicated to keeping the town clean.

Hirshberg hasn't forgotten his humble beginnings. Determined to help other people out there with an idea and ambition to succeed, each year he hosts the Stonyfield Farm Entre-

preneurship Institute. Venture capitalists, entrepreneurs and people who want to be entrepreneurs come out to a two-day conference to hear industry leaders, including Hirshberg, tell how they struggled, but eventually succeeded.

Those with a dream for starting their own business also get a chance to have their idea reviewed and discussed by other entrepreneurs. Using the experience he gained all those years ago in the barn in Wilton, Hirshberg provides for them an example that having a vision and investing hard work toward it can create success.

As they look toward the future, the folks at Stonyfield, at heart, are still the same idealists they were back in that leaky barn and they still see room for growth.

While they have watched the percentage of the organic grocery market grow from 2 percent to 4 percent of overall food sales over the past several years, they want to see that increase.

Stonyfield believes the best way to grow the demand for organic is through education, so part of the company's mission is to teach people what it means to farm organically and that eating organic foods is an investment in health for humans and the planet. With that increased demand comes a loyalty that could put organic on par with conventional agriculture.

And New Hampshire is the place to bring that dream to fruition.

"As one of the largest employers in the state, Stonyfield is honored to represent New Hampshire's manufacturing sector, a critical part of our economy that has taken a beating in recent decades as more and more production has moved offshore," Hirshberg said. "Clearly New Hampshire and America have built our economic strength on our ability to produce the things that people want to consume."

Samuel Kaymen and Gary Hirshberg in the beginning

Even with all of its success, the core values of the company have never wavered: Help family farms survive, help the planet, promote and educate the public on the benefits of organic, and to do it all in New Hampshire.

TURBOCAM International

The TURBOCAM team gathers in front of its corporate headquarters in Barrington.
Inset: TURBOCAM founder and president Marian B. Noronha

When manufacturers of high-performance turbomachinery applications need five-axis machining, they think of TURBOCAM. With over 150 CNC milling machines at 11 locations in nine countries on four continents, TURBOCAM has quickly become one of the world's largest suppliers of five-axis machined impellers and blades.

TURBOCAM, for TURBOmachinery Computer Aided Manufacturing, was founded in 1985 by Marian Noronha, who grew up in India. In 1962, he witnessed the U.S. Air Force delivering supplies to help his people ravaged by the Sino-Indian War. At 8 years old, he decided he wanted to become a part of such a generous country and also felt he had a debt to repay. He eventually immigrated here in 1979.

After completing some graduate studies in mechanical engineering and a few years as a windmill engineer in Vermont, Mr. Noronha settled in the Seacoast area in 1983. Borrowing money from family and friends, he started TURBOCAM as a software applications company in Madbury in September of 1985.

While its mission was committed to paper and refined several years later, TURBOCAM was birthed with a DNA of unchangeable ideals.

"Our mission statement is what drives us as a company," Mr. Noronha said. "Our purpose is to honor God, create wealth for our employees and support Christian service to God and people. We do this by achieving excellence in the manufacturing of turbomachinery parts by 5-axis machining and related

at the same time developing expertise in 5-axis programming, primarily for rotating bladed parts. In 1987, the company incorporated and bought a small BostoMatic 5-axis milling machine. One year later, TURBOCAM grew and rented space in Dover, where the business began to grow.

In 1988, the company prototyped impellers for the smallest turbo air compressor in the industry, a 125hp machine, and helped to produce a highly efficient machine. Soon these game-changing impellers found their way into larger air compressors for several manufacturers. With better aerodynamic designs and improved dynamic balance, these impellers challenged the cast wheels that were traditionally used in the industry. These new impellers were built on the metal properties of forged bar or billet instead of castings.

TURBOCAM India was launched in 1989 in Goa to meet demands for turbomachinery products in India and to build a base for job and wealth creation. TURBOCAM Europe was introduced the next year in Fareham, England. Both companies received challenging assignments, developed advanced skills and attracted loyal customers in their respective countries and regions.

Just one year later, TURBOCAM brashly contracted to make four stages of shrouded blisks for development of the Boeing 777 engines. The manufacture of these incredibly difficult parts taxed every resource of the company in software, machining skills and in machine design and maintenance. Ten months later, the capabilities of the company advanced greatly, preparing it for bigger challenges. During this same period, the company made two blisks and two stators for a small experimental aero engine. The customer claimed that the blades were perfect, with zero deviation from the nominal. Several engineers from that company later moved on to other employers, bringing more customers and projects with them as they continued to rave about TURBOCAM quality.

Now, with experienced manufacturing facilities in the United States, England and India, TURBOCAM has grown to combine the finest equipment and personnel to produce a wide range of parts for jet engines, missile systems, helicopters, satellites, rocket turbopumps and space shuttles. From producing one inch to 40-inch diameters and from developing single-piece prototypes to 1,000 piece scheduled production runs, TURBOCAM is a leading manufacturer for some of the most critical parts in aerospace—parts that simply must not fail.

TURBOCAM learned to elegantly harness computer technology to produce efficient and reliable processes that translate customer data into beautifully finished parts. Faster computers further reduced programming and machining time, while advanced software and programming expertise increased the reliability of the process. By 2000, a market developed for high volumes of turbocharger compressor impellers for truck and passenger car applications. TURBOCAM responded with its Automated Production Systems (TAPS) division, designed to

technologies and satisfying the needs of our customers for quality, price, delivery, and service. As we interact with our customers, suppliers and employees, we hold ourselves accountable to God's law as expressed in the Bible. We are committed to integrity in our business and personal relationships.

"Our mission is a statement of who we are, and why we exist," he said. "It has guided our company policies and our behavior as we have expanded from 25 people in 1993 to well over 450 in 2012. There are many ways to achieve success in business. I have learned that in a business, God comes first. God has blessed our efforts and made us a growing company with dedicated employees, loyal customers and many suppliers who enjoy being associated with us."

The early years saw TURBOCAM create many software solutions for manufacturing within different applications, while

TURBOCAM is a leading manufacturer for some of the most critical parts in aerospace - parts that simply must not fail.

TURBOCAM specializes in the manufacture of impellers via 5-axis milling for aerospace, industrial, and automotive applications.

TURBOCAM (continued)

TURBOCAM has over 150 milling centers at 11 locations in nine countries on four continents.

work around the clock while fully unmanned on Sundays.

"Sunday is a time of rest and so we automated our facility by purchasing robots that do the work for us," said Mr. Noronha. "Our facility is what is often called a 'lights out' factory. It runs 24/7 and it can run without people, as long as the machines are properly set up. So, Sunday can be as productive as any other day, but without anyone in the building."

In 2004, a new plant was built in Barrington and the division grew to make over 400,000 impellers per year. Similar numbers of turbine nozzles are also produced at TAPS. These products have enabled TURBOCAM's customer to achieve goals of emissions reductions ahead of its competitors and significantly increase market share.

Becoming a world-class leader in 5-axis machining doesn't happen overnight.

"There has been a lot of hard work to get to this point and it has not always been good times in our industry," Mr. Noronha said.

In 2008, TURBOCAM was thriving and sales were at $60 million despite many challenges in the local and national economy. But that all changed in 2009. The stock market tumbled, many lending institutions went bankrupt and the housing market boom at the time came to a halt. The economy was in trouble.

"Our sales were down and we were faced with a possible layoff," he said. "Having to choose between keeping the business afloat or taking away a person's livelihood is a really tough decision. We chose to be creative instead."

By being creative, TURBOCAM found a way to keep people employed while volatile economic factors resulted in a temporary decline in sales. TURBOCAM achieved this by reassigning some of its idle employees to the Phase III building project. Construction on Phase I, the Automated Production Systems division, was completed in 2004 and Phase II, the Industrials division, was completed just two years later. In 2008, construction on Phase III began. TURBOCAM had hired a construction company, but opted to manage the project internally and reassigned interested employees as construction laborers. Many jobs were saved and business picked up again later that year.

Throughout the years, TURBOCAM and Mr. Noronha have received numerous awards, such as "Supplier of the Year," "Inc. 5000 List of Fastest Growing Companies" and *Business New Hampshire Magazine's* "2009 Business Leader of the Year." One of the most prestigious awards TURBOCAM received was the Freedom Award in 2007. The award was created by the Department of Defense to recognize employers providing exceptional support to their National Guard and Reserve employees. It is the highest in a series of employer recognition awards given by the agency.

TURBOCAM provided one of its National Guardsmen on a tour of duty with software and hardware to allow Internet cafe capabilities for his unit, while another employee's unit was provided with life-saving battlefield surveillance technology. The company also established a $10,000 fund so its deployed employees could draw from it when vital supplies were not readily available through normal channels. Wall displays, company publications and newsletters all pay tribute to the company's military employees.

Today, TURBOCAM divisions have also emerged in the Netherlands, Taiwan, Romania, Japan and South Africa. They supply a variety of products to the steam and gas turbine markets, manage complex supply chains and are an international liaison. An affiliated company, CAMplete Solutions Inc. in Canada, provides software solutions, packaging some of the best manufacturing practices from TURBOCAM.

Bold and creative solutions to design and manufacturing challenges, combined with understanding economic constraints and international opportunities, have characterized TURBOCAM's culture. No less significant has been the determination to follow the company's mission.

"While TURBOCAM has done well, we continue to believe that it is more important that we do good," Mr. Noronha said. "Honoring God and supporting Christian service to God and people comes first and TURBOCAM supports several projects around the world that demonstrate this commitment."

Since its inception, TURBOCAM has provided extensive support to orphanages, locally and abroad. One of them, El Shaddai Child Rescue House in India, is now caring for over 600 children. TURBOCAM's financial support helps to provide food, shelter, clothing, school fees, and basic medical care.

Another endeavor that TURBOCAM founded and directs is called "Bridge to Nepal." In 1998, after learning about Nepali "kamaiyas," or slaves, Mr. Noronha made his first trip to Nepal in 1999 with the mission of freeing slaves and their families from their generational bondage and debt. Working with two Nepali men, he freed seven families in 1999 and 35 more families in 2000. Today, TURBOCAM and its employees make numerous trips every year to Nepal to provide livestock, support orphanages, provide clean drinking water, school supplies and more. Education is key to improving the future for ex-slave families in Nepal. By raising a generation of educated children, society will begin to break the cycle of illiteracy and ultimately improve the overall standard of living. Toward that end, TURBOCAM funded the construction of four schools now serving hundreds of children, with a fifth to be completed in 2012.

In the developing world, water quality remains a major concern. Children under five years old make up over 90 percent of the 42,000 deaths that occur every week from unsafe water and unhygienic living conditions. Many of these diseases are preventable. TURBOCAM is working to provide safe water — liquid hope — to those who have none, both in developing countries and disaster areas. Through one-of-a-kind engineering innovations and in partnership with other organizations, TURBOCAM is helping to transform communities and change lives every day in Nepal, India, Africa and several other regions through the gift of clean water.

From the space shuttle to jet engines, from electric power generation to gas pipelines, from automotive turbochargers to marine propellers, from air refrigeration chillers to artificial heart pumps, from redeeming slaves in Nepal to building orphanages in India, TURBOCAM products and missions touch lives in New Hampshire and around the world every day.

In 1998, after learning about Nepali "kamaiyas," or slaves, Mr. Noronha made his first trip to Nepal in 1999 with the mission of freeing slaves and their families from their generational bondage and debt.

TURBOCAM's Automated Production Systems division runs 24/7, but is fully unmanned on Sundays. It produces nearly one million impellers and nozzle rings annually.

New Hampshire Motor Speedway

New Hampshire Motor Speedway is a destination attraction for more than 600,000 visitors every year, who come trackside to fulfill their own need for speed.

In New Hampshire Motor Speedway's world, the commute to work is 300 miles and the traffic is always bumper-to-bumper. In the speedway's world, driving speeds reach 165 mph just before a sharp left or a pit stop. That is all before the route changes and motorcycles come to town for even faster speeds.

New Hampshire Motor Speedway is a destination attraction for more than 600,000 visitors every year, who come trackside to fulfill their own need for speed. The 1,100-acre multi-use complex in Loudon is the largest sports and entertainment facility in New England, with a capacity for 105,491 spectators.

New England's beloved speedway hosts two coveted NASCAR Sprint Cup Series race weekends each year, one of which is a championship playoff race. Big name drivers, including Jimmie Johnson, Jeff Gordon, Kyle Busch and teammates Ryan Newman and Tony Stewart, have all celebrated wins in this Victory Lane.

Nationally-televised events mean millions of people can witness all the sights and sounds of a race weekend, putting a spotlight on the Granite State. Sprint Cup weekends are the preeminent sporting events in New Hampshire each summer, but they are hardly the only excitement for fans who speed through the gates.

"The Magic Mile" hosts racing from April through October, featuring vintage racing and car shows, motorcycles, various auto clubs and racing school events. The engines are hot and the track is full virtually every day of the spring,

summer and fall, including the parking lots and other areas of this multi-use facility.

New Hampshire Motor Speedway is a major racing hub in New England, a far cry from the humble beginnings of a small dirt track opened by a handful of local race fans. It took the vision of an extraordinary man to create the high-octane environment millions enjoy today.

Like a modern day Kevin Costner with his own Field of Dreams, Bob Bahre, a New England businessman, had that vision in 1989 to bring big-time NASCAR racing to the Northeast. He was confident New Hampshire was already a hotbed of racing with passionate fans that would support major events. He imagined that if he built it, they would come.

Bahre centered his sights on Bryar Motorsports Park in Loudon. Geographically, he believed Loudon was in a prime location, with easy access to the White Mountains and the Lakes Region; Boston, Mass.; Providence, R.I; the rest of New England and even Canada, which boasts an enthusiastic racing audience.

Bryar Motorsports Park was originally opened in 1960 as a go-kart track and was a glorified playground for racers when Bahre arrived. The track underwent many transformations, from a 1/5-mile dirt track to a 5/8-mile paved oval. In 1989, the fate of racing in Loudon was sealed with a real estate deal.

That year, Bahre, along with his brother, Dick, and son, Gary, purchased the short track and began turning their vision into a reality. With an investment of heart and soul, and a lot of construction and renovations, the Bahre family built New Hampshire International Speedway, a 1.058-mile oval and 1.6-mile road course, in 1990.

So he built it and they came - in huge numbers - beyond anyone's expectations.

In its current incarnation, New Hampshire Motor Speedway, now owned by Speedway Motorsports, Inc., is a magnet for hundreds of thousands of race fans every year, creating a major economic engine for the Granite State, pumping more than $400 million dollars in tourism spending into the state's economy every single year.

Under the SMI umbrella, headed by chairman Bruton Smith, the company owns seven speedways throughout the country, in addition to New Hampshire. In the Granite State, it employs 30 people full-time and 1,500 part-time at the height of the racing season.

Since the SMI purchase from the Bahre family for $340 million in 2008, there have been many upgrades to the track. Expanded RV spaces, infield reconfiguration for increased usable space and functionality, the installation of an enhanced trackside safety fence and increased directional signage were a few of the upgrades immediately completed.

A massive new bathhouse, the Frank Webb Bath Center, was built for the nearly 10,000 campers on site each year and added 30 shower stalls and 30 toilets, for the most expensive bathroom in New Hampshire.

An amenity also enhancing the fan experience is the $1.2 million state-of-the-art scoreboard, boasting three 32-foot-by-18-foot Panasonic TV screens and a scrolling leaderboard with color graphics that gives fans running positions and lap times for all 43 drivers.

That culture spreads beyond the gates of "The Magic Mile." Each year, the speedway family gives back to those who

make racing so successful in New Hampshire by donating $1 million to local non-profit groups and children-related charities. The New Hampshire Chapter of Speedway Children's Charities serves underprivileged children throughout New England and benefits more than 12,000 children each year.

"Fans First" is the speedway's motto. It embodies the goal of serving the community, bringing in new events, improving amenities and creating a year-round destination for family entertainment. This is what keeps the speedway on track for future growth.

Racing is all about moving forward and New Hampshire Motor Speedway will continue to strive to provide the most exciting racing the region has ever seen.

Buckle up New England - it's going to be a great ride.

Smuttynose Brewing Company

David Yarrington, Director of Brewing Operations at Smuttynose, holding office hours.

Bob Lussier Photography

Whether it's in turn of the century work-a-day pubs, deliciously illicit speakeasies, or the modern sensibility of a microbrewery, America's love affair with beer has stood the test of time and the local brews from The Portsmouth Brewery, the Granite State's original brewpub, and Smuttynose Brewing, one of the country's most highly-regarded craft breweries, are New Hampshire's best sweethearts.

Both companies have their own personalities, which are a reflection of their owners, Peter Egelston and Joanne Francis, and their dedicated employees. They have marched to their own beat, even when choices they made cost more money or were contrary to conventional wisdom.

It's not only worked, but served them well. Playing no small role in the story of Smuttynose and the Portsmouth Brewery is the Granite State itself.

"One of the things that I have always appreciated about New Hampshire is the scale of it," Egelston said. "It's a small state and the level of access people of New Hampshire have to each other, to the policy makers, to local and state representatives is valuable. Having that kind of personal access helps to get things done."

The Portsmouth Brewery was founded in 1991 and Smuttynose in 1994, but the companies' roots go back to 1987 when Egelston and his sister, Janet, along with two other partners, opened their first brewpub, the Northampton Brewery, in western Massachusetts. At that time, the legacy of Prohibition and World War II had winnowed the number of breweries in the U.S. from 2,000 in the 19th century to about 30, all producing what was essentially the same product. At the time of its opening, the Northampton Brewery was one of only several dozen brewpubs in the entire nation, with only a handful on the East Coast.

For most people back then, a brewpub was a very unfamiliar, even strange idea, and there was no guarantee that this idea would catch on. Nonetheless, for pioneer craft brewers, the notion of locally made, handcrafted beer intuitively made sense. In retrospect, given the ongoing evolution of consumer values and habits, the emergence of craft beer seems obvious, almost inevitable, in fact. But it was far from clear back in 1987 when the Egelstons opened their doors to their first curious customers, many of whom wrinkled their noses after experiencing a full-flavored beer for the first time. Much like the artisanal bakeries, which were introducing traditional breads to a nation weaned on white bread around the same time, they had their work cut out for them.

Within a year after opening the Northampton Brewery, the Egelstons began searching for a location for a second brewpub, and in 1990 they found a site in Portsmouth that met all their requirements. They were smitten with the quirky city, which wasn't the vibrant hub it has become, but it was lively and had a thriving restaurant and bar scene. It was hip without knowing it, was on the cusp of a hot arts scene emerging and its economy was awful.

It was perfect.

Egelston was not dissuaded by those who urged him to go somewhere else. They pointed out that the Pease Air Force base had just closed down and the Portsmouth Naval Shipyard was cutting back. Jobs were disappearing and people were following them, taking with them beer money.

Nonetheless, the Egelston siblings saw a great opportunity. Aside from the charms of Portsmouth, part of New Hampshire's lure was its favorable legal climate when it came to beer and breweries. The other upside of the bleak economy was the availability of inexpensive real estate right in the downtown. With all that wasn't happening in the city, there was nowhere to go but up. They purchased a building on Market Street in downtown Portsmouth and in June 1991, opened the Portsmouth Brewery, the first brewpub and craft brewery in New Hampshire.

Three years later, they bought the building next door to the original shop at 56 Market St., allowing expansion of the restaurant and kitchen and the addition of a small gift shop and beer garden.

For most people back then, a brewpub was a very unfamiliar, even strange idea, and there was no guarantee that this idea would catch on.

Below: The fermentation cellar at Smuttynose is crowded with tanks of all sizes.

Bob Lussier Photography

From milling the grain to making the mash through the fermenting process, the brewers take the pride of craftsmen in every step of the process, made by hand using traditional methods and ingredients.

Tod Mott, Head Brewer at the Portsmouth Brewery, offering one of his signature beers.

Dan Gair/Blind Dog Photo

The Portsmouth Brewery, which employs 85 people, led by general manager Brennen Rumble, Chef Todd Sweet and Head Brewer Tod Mott, is well-known in the region for its charitable work and involvement in community affairs. It has also become a leader in sustainable business practices and features locally-produced foods on its menu whenever possible.

The Portsmouth Brewery's brewers make three to four batches a week, seven barrels -or 217 gallons - at a time, producing about 1,200 barrels, or 300,000 pints of beer annually, From milling the grain to making the mash through the fermenting process, the brewers take the pride of craftsmen in every step of the process, made by hand using traditional methods and ingredients. Each beer begins with just water, malted barley, hops and yeast. Exceptions to this are wheat beers, which use malted wheat and barley and some seasonal beers, which may be brewed with fruits and spices, depending on the time of year.

During the early 1990s, the craft brewing industry, though still in its infancy, was growing rapidly, and the Egelstons, now operators of two successful brewpubs, began to contemplate the possibility of expanding beyond their brewpub business and into wholesale production of packaged beer. Since neither of their pub breweries had the capacity for this kind of production, it was clear that a larger facility would be necessary. An opportunity arose sooner than either had anticipated in late 1993, when the Frank Jones Brewing Company, a small microbrewery that had opened in Portsmouth in 1992, went bankrupt and the company's assets went up for auction. Peter Egelston attended the auction and although the bids that day did not meet the bank's minimum requirement, Egelston sub-

sequently formed an impromptu partnership with the owners of another small brewery to submit a sealed bid with the notion of reopening and jointly operating the facility under a different name. Theirs, it turned out, was the winning bid, and in January 1994, Egelston held the key to what would become Smuttynose Brewing Company.

Because these events had unfolded so quickly, there had been no time to develop a business plan, a marketing plan or even to name the company. Peter Egelston suggested 'Smuttynose,' taking the name of a small island off the coast of Portsmouth, believing that it had a strong local resonance and was unusual enough to become a memorable brand name. Several former Frank Jones brewers were hired to get the brewery up and running, and in January 1994, Smuttynose Brewing Company came to life. Within a month of the original purchase of the Frank Jones equipment, Egelston concluded that he had a very different vision for the new business than his new partners did, so he bought them out.

Several months later, in July 1994, Smuttynose celebrated the debut of its first beer, Shoals Pale Ale, which was tapped at a local Portsmouth restaurant. That fall, Old Brown Dog Ale was added to the lineup and the brewery released its first bottled beers. Over time, more new products were introduced, including a Variety 12-pack - still the company's biggest selling item - and the Big Beer Series, consisting of limited-release editions of full-bodied, robust beer styles, such as Imperial Stout and Barleywine. Since the very start, Smuttynose has focused on traditional and sometimes little-known beer styles, beers with a lot of character, often hopped aggressively and stronger than typical domestic beers, confident that beer lovers would embrace these styles.

In 2000, Janet and Peter Egelston ended their partnership. Janet retained ownership of their original brewpub, the Northampton Brewery, and Peter, with his partner, Joanne Francis, kept the two companies in New Hampshire. In 2000, David Yarrington became an assistant brewer and is now Director of Brewing Operations, bringing a level of professionalism and creativity that is second to none in the industry. Other key personnel include sales manager Kevin Love, who joined the company in 1997; Greg Blanchard, the head brewer at Smuttynose since 1998, and business manager Gale Merrigan, who started at the Northampton Brewery in 1991 before becoming a member of the Portsmouth Brewery's original management team.

Smuttynose outgrew "microbrewery" status in 2006, when annual production exceeded 15,000 barrels. Its beers are sold in 18 states, distributed by a network of 38 wholesalers. The expansion of the company's territorial footprint has been slow and steady, with growth based on consumer demand and the brewery's ability to service new markets. Smuttynose is guided by the belief that craft brewing was, and always will be, primarily a regional phenomenon. The company's long-term goal is to consolidate its reputation as one of America's finest small, regional breweries and to lead the industry in product quality, creativity and the responsible stewardship of its business.

In recent years, the greatest challenge facing Smuttynose has been keeping up with growing demand. In late 2011, construction began on a new facility in Hampton, about 10 miles south of the company's present location, which will double the brewery's capacity. This will be a LEED-certified facility, in keeping with the company's goals of sustainability and responsible stewardship.

Although not yet a household name, Smuttynose was recently ranked 20th out of more than 5,000 breweries rated on Beer Advocate magazine's list of "All-Time Top Breweries on Planet Earth." It was also rated 28th on Rate Beer's list of 2011 Best Brewers in the World, out of more than 10,000 breweries reviewed.

Going forward, the company's mission is much as it has always been. The Portsmouth Brewery takes very seriously its role as a public house, in the best sense of the word, believing its future is tied to its continued focus on contributing to the community and serving as a gathering place for people of all ages and persuasions.

As a 20-something year-old restaurant, the Portsmouth Brewery must steer a course between being familiar and comfortable to long-time patrons, while constantly looking for ways to stay fresh and interesting to all of its customers.

As for Smuttynose, its vision is to remain a small, regionally-based artisanal brewer with strong local support, a reputation for creating and serving fine beers, and continuing it efforts to become a more responsible, sustainable company.

"Over the years, we have been blessed with the hard work of many talented and devoted individuals who have put a good deal of their own energy into promoting, preserving and evolving our mission," Egelston said. "Without our people, we'd be nowhere."

Although not yet a household name, Smuttynose was recently ranked 20th out of more than 5,000 breweries ...

Michael Winters

Executive Chef Todd Sweet and his kitchen warriors.

FIRST® | For Inspiration and Recognition of Science and Technology

FIRST is a competitive "Sport for the Mind™"; a fun, creative, hands-on learning experience to inspire future scientists and engineers.

Since its founding, FIRST has grown into an international phenomenon, introducing hundreds of thousands of participants to the challenges and rewards of science and engineering.

More than 20 years ago, inventor Dean Kamen, president of DEKA Research & Development Corp. in Manchester, visited the SEE Science Center, an interactive museum he had founded in the Queen City's old Millyard. After a conversation with visiting students, he was surprised at their lack of enthusiasm for the crucial disciplines of science and mathematics.

That became the inspiration for *FIRST*® (For Inspiration and Recognition of Science and Technology), a non-profit organization he founded in 1989 that combines the thrill of competition and the excitement of robotics to change how youth views science, technology, math and engineering..

Through a series of robotics competitions for children of all ages, *FIRST* offers a hands-on scientific adventure. Junior *FIRST*® LEGO® League and *FIRST*® LEGO® League give elementary and middle school students the opportunity to examine a real-world issue by interviewing experts and employing LEGO elements. High schoolers can choose between the *FIRST*® Tech Challenge or the organization's flagship program, the *FIRST*® Robotics Competition, in which 120-pound ro-

bots compete on a field the size of a basketball court.

FIRST learning never stops. From age 6 to 18, the programs help students master skills and concepts they will use following the *FIRST* path from one level to the next and beyond, through college and their career. In addition to gaining real, hands-on experience in engineering and programming as they design and build working robots, *FIRST* participants also discover the business side of technology, such as conducting research, obtaining patents, creating a company, raising capital and executing marketing programs.

From its inception, only a very few imagined a program combining the imperative need for science education with the excitement and exhilaration of a competitive sport would endure After more than two decades, *FIRST* has done just that.

The key is a magical combination of the expertise of professional scientists and engineers, the passion of great teachers, the energy of dedicated parents, the power of visionary political leaders and the incredible enthusiasm of the next generation of innovators that show students that indeed, anything is possible.

Since its founding, *FIRST* has grown into an international phenomenon, introducing hundreds of thousands of participants to the challenges and rewards of science and engineering. Each year, 100,000 mentors and volunteers donate their time and expertise to show students how rewarding careers in science can be, while the nation's top colleges and universities offer nearly $14 million in scholarships. More than 3,000 of the world's leading corporations and foundations, from BAE Systems and Boeing to Google, Microsoft and jcpenney, supply resources and sponsorships to help *FIRST* participants' dreams become a reality.

FIRST alumni are more likely to attend college, study engineering and pursue careers in science and technology, according to a Brandeis University study. US presidents honor FIRST Championship winners at the White House. They are also celebrated in their communities as true innovators.

In 1992, at a high school in Manchester, *FIRST* held its inaugural competition, consisting of 28 teams in a small gymnasium, creating an institution that would fundamentally change the way students see and experience science and technology.

Although FIRST teams can now be found throughout the world, the organization maintains close ties to the Granite State. Its headquarters occupy one of Manchester's famed mill buildings, bridging the Industrial Revolution of the city's past with its future as a hub for technological innovation. Each year, business leaders and political officials flock to Southern New Hampshire University for the *FIRST* Robotics Competition Kickoff event. The BAE Systems/Granite State Regional event, held in the Verizon Wireless Arena, is an unmatched celebration of competition and achievement.

Of the many groundbreaking technologies Kamen has developed, *FIRST* may be his proudest creation of all.

"Ten years from today, one of these students is going to be out in the world having done something extraordinary for a major, global problem," he said.

Whatever new challenges the future may present, the young innovators of *FIRST* will be there to find a solution and change the world.

Each year, 100,000 mentors and volunteers donate their time and expertise to show students how rewarding careers in science can be, while the nation's top colleges and universities offer nearly $14 million in scholarships.

Photos: Adriana M. Groisman

BAE Systems

BAE Systems, founded in Nashua, has grown to 5,000 employees working in five locations in New Hampshire.

Its products are used everywhere, from major U.S. metropolitan areas to Afghanistan to Earth's orbit and even on Mars.

In the last 60 years, BAE Systems in Nashua has evolved from a company of 200 employees renting the top two floors of a former textile mill to one with 13,000 locations all over the world.

In 1952, Royden Sanders founded the technology firm with a simple goal of doing "really good engineering." That year, he and 10 other colleagues put up $5,000 each – some even putting second mortgages on their homes to do so – to establish the company, then known as Sanders Associates.

The genesis of Sanders Associates reflected the economic climate of the surrounding area. The company, in its first few years, did not have a record of success and had to build its track record by taking on small subcontracts on other companies' larger programs. At the same time, in the early 1950s, Nashua's textile industry was in its decline and by the end of that decade, the company bought the former Jackson Mill, began winning larger contracts and employed 1,500 people.

Nearly 5,000 employees work at BAE System's five locations in New Hampshire. Its products are used everywhere, from major U.S. metropolitan areas to Afghanistan to Earth's orbit and even on Mars. Time and again, the company is lauded for its role in ushering in the age of high technology into New Hampshire.

As the company grew, its commitment to the community where its employees live and work never diminished. Over the years, BAE Systems has remained vigilant to its goal of giving back to the local area, offering scores of donations, sponsorships and educational programs designed to perpetuate New Hampshire's base of engineering expertise.

Recognizing the responsibility of industry leaders to help cultivate the next generation of scientists, mathematicians and engineers, BAE Systems organizes internships and mentoring and student enrichment programs to bolster young people's interest in careers in the high tech industry.

BAE Systems' support for education and philanthropic endeavors is notable. The company presented $1 million gift to the University of New Hampshire to establish an advanced technology center at the College of Engineering and Physical Sciences and its support of the McAuliffe-Shepard Discovery Center allowed expansion of the facility to better accommodate the growing programs that encourage students' interest in science and technology.

"BAE Systems' support is unparalleled in New Hampshire's business community," said Erle Pierce, vice president of Touch the Future Inc., which supports the operation of the McAuliffe-Shepard Discovery Center. "They have been a vital partner of the Discovery Center, sharing the common values of excellence and achievement that have enabled us to launch our next generation of heroes."

The company's technological ingenuity touches many aspects of daily life, from making mass transportation more environmentally friendly to ensuring that communications satellites' hardware can withstand the sun's radiation while in orbit. Every year, the company's engineers receive dozens of patent awards for their inventions.

The minds of the company even helped in the advent of a home entertainment mainstay: The personal game console. In 1966, while working at the company's Canal Street location in Nashua, Ralph Baer began developing his "Brown Box" prototype, which would become the Magnavox Odyssey, the first gaming console to play "PONG."

Innovation is a key component of BAE Systems' success and the company believes that promoting innovation is not only good for business, but for the world. To encourage young minds to think innovatively, BAE Systems became a strategic partner with the New Hampshire-based FIRST® (For Inspiration and Recognition of Science and Technology) organization, dedicating financial contributions and a large contingent of employee volunteers to help mentor youngsters as they begin exploring science and technology.

"BAE Systems has been a tremendously generous supporter of FIRST and the FIRST® Robotics Competition," said FIRST founder Dean Kamen. "As a strategic partner, BAE Systems greatly helps us to achieve our vision: 'To create a world where science and technology are celebrated ... where young people dream of becoming science and technology leaders.'"

BAE Systems is a global company with a local mind, engaging with nonprofit organizations to provide support and opportunities for employees to be involved in their communities. Whether by volunteering for events like the United Way of Greater Nashua's Day of Caring or through contributing

The employees at BAE Systems provide generous support to the local community, volunteering their time for local charity organizations.

to BAE Systems' Charity Challenge supporting organizations like the American Red Cross, American Cancer Society and the New Hampshire-based Easter Seals Veterans Count Club, BAE Systems employees are an integral part of the communities where they live and work.

Easter Seals New Hampshire officials praise BAE Systems and its employees for making "a tremendous difference to our clients," by "employing a corporate giving philosophy and encouraging community volunteerism from their employees."

BAE Systems in New Hampshire began as a small startup company with a simple idea. Over the last six decades, it has expanded to become one of the largest employers in the Granite State, while never forgetting how much the local community has given the company throughout the years. Knowing that it can only be as strong as its local community, BAE Systems has devoted numerous contributions and volunteer hours to enhance New Hampshire's educational and cultural organizations and will continue working to foster a strong, innovative engineering base in the Granite State for generations to come.

Over the years, BAE Systems has remained vigilant to its goal of giving back to the local area, offering scores of donations, sponsorships and educational programs designed to perpetuate New Hampshire's base of engineering expertise.

Nanocomp Technologies

NASA's Juno mission to Jupiter launched in August, 2011. Nanocomp Technologies' CNT material is prominently installed on the spacecraft's attitude control motor struts and main engine housing to provide electrostatic discharge protection often encountered in the rigorous environment of space.

Photos this page: NASA

For years, carbon nanotubes, or CNTs, were hailed as the next great advance in materials technology based on their "miraculous" properties of superior strength, highly-efficient electrical and thermal conductivity, and ultra-light weight. As promising as the technology has been, no commercial manufacturer or academic developer was able to capture their attractive nanoscale properties in a way that could be used by existing industrial processes at meaningful scale.

But Concord's Nanocomp Technologies has done just that and the company is the world's leader in making that claim reality.

In 2003, material scientist David Lashmore, Ph.D., was a researcher at a small technology development firm in Lebanon. In the course of his experiments, he conceived a breakthrough method for producing very long, very pure CNTs. For decades, nanotubes were generally produced in the form of a powder, with poor macro-properties that made them difficult to incorporate into useful products. This was a significant problem holding back their development.

Long CNTs solved those issues. By 2011, Lashmore's foundational work in long CNTs would be the basis for a material praised by the United States Department of Defense as "critical for national defense capabilities."

Today, Lashmore is Chief Technology Officer of Nanocomp and together with co-founder and CEO Peter Antoinette, the company is putting New Hampshire on the map as the leader in next-generation nanotechnology manufacturing, enhancing the local economy and the country's global competitiveness.

In an ironic twist, the company borrows from New Hampshire's history and the era of the textile industry, "spinning" its long carbon nanotubes into a material that resembles yarn or thread. This offers revolutionary performance advantages over many existing materials available today such as copper. Nanocomp's CTex™ yarns are extremely light, strong and can simultaneously conduct electricity and heat, while at the same time, are impervious to corrosion or sunlight degradation.

The company also produces its nanotubes as a "sheet" material, which comes out of the production system resembling a black tarpaulin and carries the same astonishing structural and conductive properties as the yarns.

Together, the yarn and sheet materials form the building blocks for a number of value-added industrial products falling into several key categories. As electrical conductors, the company's materials serve as electrical wire, cables, antenna and windings for electric motors. In addition, they can perform as enhanced composites for structural and armor applications. The material is stronger than steel but 60 percent lighter than aluminum and strong enough to stop a 9MM bullet with a stacked piece of its material. Nanocomp promises to save lives of military ground forces and law enforcement with armor applications.

Nanocomp's CNT materials are being used in space, functioning as a lightweight electrical shield blocking electromagnetic interference, electrostatic discharge and the effects from solar or electromagnetic pulses. NASA used Nanocomp's EMSHIELD™ material on the 2011 Juno spacecraft as a lightweight surface layer on critical components, including the support struts for the attitude control thrusters and the main engine housing.

The company sees significant interest in it for use in aerospace, where lightweight EMI shielding, wiring and composites will have a material impact in enhancing performance of military aircraft or saving fuel in commercial airliners.

Power systems, including batteries cables, motors and thermoelectric heat engines, show great potential for CNT use. Nanocomp's multiple properties, both independently and in combination, may be the next clean energy solution in generation, storage, transmission and efficiency. Strong lightweight wires and structures reduce expensive fuel costs in air, land and marine transportation applications. CNT sheet-based waste-heat recapture systems can transform heat losses to energy gains. Sheet systems also offer the potential to increase the generation and storage capacity of today's lithium batteries. Some view the Nanocomp wire as the next generation transmission wire to provide fast, lightweight and strong "smart grid" solutions.

A 400-foot roll of Nanocomp Technologies' EMSHIELD™ CNT sheet product being prepared for delivery to a major customer.

Perhaps of greatest significance are applications in which Nanocomp's CNTs serve many functions with one material. For example, on an aircraft wing, the company's CNT sheets can act simultaneously as an EMI shield; a de-icer; a lightning strike protector; a strengthening layer or even an embedded conductor, replacing the need for wires throughout the wing without adding significant weight to the plane.

The combination of high-strength, light weight, and electrical and thermal conductivity is a materials advancement that compares to the commercialization of aluminum in at the turn of the 19th century, or carbon fiber in the 1950s.

Presently, Nanocomp is the only US producer of such an array of CNT materials with the properties and scale and potential to be the strongest, lightest and most conductive material on earth.

In 2010, Antoinette was one of 11 experts selected for President Obama's Council of Advisors on Science and Technology, an advisory group of the nation's leading scientists and engineers that makes policy recommendations to Congress on a range of issues relating to science, technology and innovation.

Nanocomp has 45 employees and operates three production shifts daily in its 11,000 square-foot-facility and to accommodate demand for its product, a 100,000-square-foot facility has been added in Merrimack. Brought online in 2012, this facility will employ hundreds of additional employees and have the capability to produce 10 metric tons of carbon nanotube sheet and yarn products annually. This, company officials expect, will be first of many additional nano-manufacturing facilities in the US, Europe and Asia.

Nobody in the world has achieved what Nanocomp has and the company expects to extend its market lead through the 21st century and beyond.

For Nanocomp Technologies and New Hampshire, the sky is the limit.

Presently, Nanocomp is the only US producer of such an array of CNT materials with the properties and scale and potential to be the strongest, lightest and most conductive material on earth.

Company Index

NEW HAMPSHIRE: FIRST IN THE NATION

Contributing Photographers

David Brownell

David Brownell is best known for his outdoor sports and recreation photography, characterized by stop-action timing and unique use of outdoor lighting. An award winning photographer with 30 years of experience and extensive travel around the world, Brownell's photos have graced the covers of hundreds of magazines, including *Yankee, National Geographic World, Powder* and *Snow Country*. A former contributing editor to *Outdoor Photographer*, Brownell has conducted photo seminars. The producers of the PBS series, *The Great Outdoors*, selected him to host the photography segments.

Jim Carlen

Jim Carlen is a fine art nature/landscape photographer whose images of the Granite State have appeared in several regional publications, including *Manchester Magazine* and *New England Bride*. He has been a professional wedding and portrait photographer since 1994. He is a member of Professional Photographers of America and New Hampshire Professional Photographers of America, where he has won several awards at the annual NHPPA print competition. He lives in Amherst with his wife and two daughters.

Phil Cohen

Phil Cohen is a lifelong New Englander, and as a Portsmouth transplant, New Hampshire's seacoast is his canvas. With his camera always within reach, he enjoys the pursuit of capturing the essence of his surroundings. His many clients include The Music Hall, the state of New Hampshire, Portsmouth Regional Hospital, The Portsmouth Chamber of Commerce, The Ale House Inn and the New Hampshire Film Festival and his work has been published in *Yankee Magazine* and *Travel & Leisure*. He lives in Portsmouth with his wife, Stephanie.

John Gill

John Gill is a professional nature and landscape photographer whose work is published regularly. In addition to assignments and providing image rights to publications, he sells prints directly to private and corporate clients through his website. The New Hampshire Professional Photographers Association has twice honored Gill as its Photographer of the Year. He and his wife, Ruth, live in Gilford and have two grown sons.

Bob Grant

A native of the Mount Washington Valley, Bob Grant has photographed New Hampshire in all its seasons since 1975. After a brief career shooting ski movies while in college in Colorado, he connected with a leading stock house in New York, which helped to broaden his traveling and photographic experiences. Grant is most inspired winter and travels once a year to other parts of the world for inspiration, but is always glad to return home to the Valley.

Currier Museum of Art

Piscataqua River Sunset, Portsmouth